Sea,
Salt
and
Solitude

CHRIS HEWITT & DEBORAH RICHARDS

Everyone, including the authors, involved in the making of this book did so without payment, enabling all profits to benefit the charity, the Fishermen's Mission.

The production costs of this book have been covered by the incredible generosity of our sponsors.

Jackie Stanley (Harbour Holidays)
Padstow Harbour Commissioners
Rick and Katie Toogood
Sharp's Brewery

The Fishermen's Mission maintains a Christian presence in the United Kingdom's fishing communities, in order to provide, regardless of race or creed, practical, welfare and spiritual support to active and retired fishermen and their families.

www.fishermensmission.org.uk

PB ISBN - 978 - 1 - 9996788 - 7 - 6
HB ISBN - 978 - 1 - 9996788 - 8 - 3

ALI GODFREY
DIRECTOR OF BUSINESS DEVELOPMENT
FISHERMEN'S MISSION

The Fishermen's Mission is the only national charity solely supporting fishermen and their families. We have been providing highly valued support, to both active and retired fishermen, around the UK coastline for more than 137 years. We receive no government or lottery funding; all our work is funded by our friends and supporters. With a long history of loyal Christian service, we are a trusted presence in an ever-changing world.

Through the decades we have provided accommodation and canteen facilities alongside hospital and medical services. In more recent years we have focussed our work through our welfare offices and 24-hour mini centres. The one consistent feature of this work is our staff. They are a recognised and trusted presence on the quayside and around ports and villages; they are seen visiting homes and making hospital visits. Crucially, we also offer 24-hour emergency support for loss of life, accidents or illness while at sea.

Welfare is the cornerstone of all we do. We have an eye to the safety and wellbeing of active fishermen in equal measure to our concerns regarding loneliness and poverty of those who have left fishing.

The South West team are keen pioneers. Having piloted a number of innovative projects; most recently the extremely successful Health Checks. Working with the NHS and other partners to provide medical tests and dental check-ups on the harbour side, for some, this has been a life saver. These checks will now be offered around the whole UK coastline.

Keith, Julian, Eddie and Ian, our South West team, are well known in the ports and coves of Cornwall, a quiet presence in the life of these communities. They ensure that we step up to help, no matter how complex or desperate the circumstances.

The seemingly never-ending goodwill, immeasurable hours of help and respect for our work is deeply touching. There are too many individuals to mention but you know who you are, words alone can never suffice to describe our deepest gratitude.

This beautiful book is the brainchild of our wonderful South West Fundraising Manager – Julian Waring. No stranger to bold ideas – his imagination and determination brought us the highly successful 'Salt of the Earth' book, unfolding the stories of the fishermen of Newlyn. This book takes you to four of Cornwall's North Coast fishing communities, Newquay, Padstow, Rock and Port Isaac. It helps you to get to know the fishermen, their families and associated people who work hard to bring fish to our plates. Nothing happens in isolation and there are people in all these places who care deeply for fishermen and their families.

I have insufficient words to offer Chris and Deborah who have photographed and spoken to the wonderful people featured in this book. I know that, like me, you will find laughter, sadness and tall stories that will fill your heart with joy.

Read on and enjoy.

FOREWORD

Over the thirty odd years I've been making television programmes I've spoken to many fishermen and always ask the same question, 'why do you love your work?' This always comes after they talk about how physically exhausting, dangerous and not always very financially rewarding a job it is, not to mention the ever-changing regulations about what they can fish and where.

The answer will invariably be something to do with the sense of peace and freedom a life at sea can offer, the solitariness of many fishermen is normally seen as a bonus. It's almost Ernest Hemingway's famous book The Old Man And The Sea repeated over and over again, there's just something about it.

I love this book in its understated stories of ordinary people who through their lives become extraordinary. Looking at the faces you realise they all have a special quality of living a fulfilled life despite having to put up with conditions the average person at their desk or computer screen could not even begin to imagine. Inevitably it goes along with such tough lives that there are, sadly, more accidents than in most other industries, so the charitable work of the Fishermen's Mission is incredibly important for these small, proud communities.

It goes without saying that without these heroes our Seafood Restaurant business would not survive, supporting the National Mission for Deep Sea Fishermen is the least we could do to express our appreciation.

CAPTAIN ROBERT ATKINSON
PADSTOW HARBOUR MASTER

Just before we went to print, Rob unexpectedly passed away.

He was instrumental in getting this book from concept to reality.
Always encouraging and supportive, he will be missed by many.

Chris, Deborah and Julian would like to dedicate this book to his memory.

CHRIS HEWITT
PHOTOGRAPHER

My Gran always taught me to be a decent human being, so it must be in there somewhere; all joking aside her influence is why I decided to get involved with this particular project.
I was approached by Julian from the Fishermen's Mission following a recommendation from a good friend of mine. "How about you take a few photos of some of the fishermen on the North Coast of Cornwall Chris?" One thousand four hundred and seventy two images later, edited down to two hundred, illustrating one hundred and forty narratives, we have a stunning document that we are very proud of, mission accomplished.

Salt of the Earth is an inspiring piece of work. To follow in David and Jan's footsteps was an enormous task. I wanted to apply my own style of documentary photography to ensure this book stood on its own two feet.

My daily photographic work tends to be landscape, fine art reproduction and product photography. Having shot many weddings I do have plenty of experience in documentary style imagery. I decided to head out into the field and record images of people in an environment they were comfortable in. By doing this subjects tend to feel a little more at ease with the camera. The most time I spent with any one subject was about three minutes.
It's a tough game photographing people who don't particularly want to be photographed.
I shot outside in all weathers in the hope of creating images that give the viewer a sense of atmosphere, time and place.

Moving back to Cornwall after thirteen years working as a stage manager, taking theatre productions on World tours, I decided it best to make use of my degree. However that got sidetracked by unintentionally opening a wine bar. Fast forward a further five years and I am now doing what I set out to do in 2003, taking photographs for a living.

I am a firm believer in Karma, you get out of life what you put in, except if you are Sally my better half, she just gets stuck with me. I have to take this opportunity to thank her for putting up with everything my hectic life throws at us both, she is a true supporter and I am very grateful. Being a Cornish boy I am happy to have been a part of something that helps an industry so entrenched in our coastal way of life.
These boys and girls risk a lot to earn a living, at the same time as putting fresh fish on our dinner plates.

I hope the money raised will continue the good work of the Fishermen's Mission.

Chris
www.chrishewittphotography.co.uk

DEBORAH RICHARDS
AUTHOR

Being born, bred and educated by Quakers it had been drummed into me that people's lives, no matter what they did, were important; there was something of God in everyone, you just had to listen. As an adult, I abandoned the religion but remained attached to many of the values. The quiet understated, practical and often invisible work of the Fishermen's Mission just appealed to the Quaker in me. I first came across the Mission while working in Grimsby forty years ago. On a chance trip to Newlyn we popped into the Mission building for a cup of tea, pictures from Salt of the Earth were displayed; this was a charity I could volunteer for now the working phase of life was over.

In 1985 I married into a prosperous mid-Cornwall farming family. They were suspicious of me, girls from the city were a threat to their future. The older generations were anxious until a male heir and two male spares arrived in quick succession. There are many parallels between farming and fishing and my experience of farming helped me gain the trust of those I interviewed and gave them some reassurance.

This project was a chance to write narrative explaining why these traditional industries feel so threatened, mis-understood and isolated. The threat comes from distant policy makers who don't 'get' remote, rural or coastal communities. The mis-understanding from a lack of knowledge of how food gets to the plate: milk comes from a cow, fish from the sea, not just from a supermarket. The isolation from a daily working life engaged with nature: her joys, her beauty, her harshness and cruelty. Having watched my brother-in-law die as a result of a farming accident with a beef animal, I knew something of the sadness and isolation of fishing tragedies.

Most of the narratives were recorded, like Chris's photographs, on location with the intention of helping people feel at ease. Transcribed using pencil and paper, some time later they were played again and the pieces written. I needed about six minutes of recording to get the number of words, some took a lot of prompting others gave sermons so long the batteries on the recorder were flat. As people relaxed, laughter, black humour and fabulous anecdotes drifted in; the best bits so often within sight of the five minute mark. I've endeavoured to use the words as they were spoken thus giving a voice to the person in the photograph.

It has been magnificent to bring together so many things I hold dear, thank you @thefishmish for asking me. I hope it raises a useful amount for you to use quietly and sensitively among these people who have welcomed me into their communities this year.

Deborah

THE FISHERMEN'S MISSION STAFF

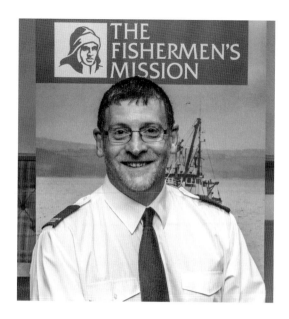

KEITH DICKSON
SENIOR SUPERINTENDENT

EDDIE FLETCHER
ADMIN ASSISTANT AND WELFARE
WORKER

JULIAN WARING
REGIONAL FUNDRAISING
MANAGER (CORNWALL)

LEN SCOTT
Len was with the Mission from 1985–2004, Senior Superintendent in Newlyn and Brixham where he was
well known and much respected.

ALBERT

Albert is the name of the Fishermen's Mission collection box. He is mentioned throughout the book as sitting among the spoons on the counter, on the shelf with the vinegar or on the bar. He was named after a retired Belgian fisherman called Albert Jansenns, who came to the UK around the time of the Second World War when mainland Europe was in turmoil. He settled in Brixham, when it was known as Little Belgium.

The cash collected in these boxes goes towards the work of The Royal National Mission to Deep Sea Fishermen, RNMDSF, commonly known as The Fishermen's Mission.

For every £1 raised 88p is spent on the services of the Charity.
In 2017 around the UK; 2,452 people received grants totalling £898,536.
Over 63 fishermen needed 24/7 emergency response.
177 fishermen received emergency response.
6,630 welfare visits to individual fishermen and their families.

Our career fishermen stand a 1 in 16 risk of losing their life in pursuit of their work.

If you would like to host Albert or help with our work in any way at all please get in touch with us
fundraising@fishermensmission.org.uk
or
Freephone 0800 634 1020

Newquay

PHIL TREBILCOCK

"…we have the oldest rowing gig in the world here, she was built in Falmouth in 1812, then there's a gap in our knowledge, we'd love to know how she came to be in Newquay…"

I've sung with Newquay Rowing Club Singers for twenty-five years. We've raised money for Children's Hospice South West, all over the county. We've sung in Ireland, Yorkshire and nineteen years ago, at the first ever gig rowing regatta at Muiden in the Netherlands.

Newquay Rowing Club is a big concern, the sport of gig rowing started here in 1921. In the 1950's the Club bought some wrecked gigs in the Scillies for restoration, £5 each! Harry Moreland of England's Glory Matchbox Co. in Gloucester was visiting William Peters a St Mawes boatbuilder, who brought him to see the old wrecks. We had the old hand skills at Brabyn's yard in Padstow but no money for the wood. Within a week he had sent a baulk of oak, one metre square by thirty or forty foot by train to the boatyard in Padstow so the work could be done.
It's all been photographed and documented too.

Of course we compete in the World Championships in the Scillies every year.

ROSS KING
FISHERMAN

"…it's much easier with family, we know the way it goes up and down, with family there's a bit less pressure than taking paid crew…"

My Grandfather was a fisherman. Dad was a fisherman till twenty years ago when family breakdown meant we lost the boat. My Northey Uncle fishes with me. When he got older we sold our individual boats and bought one together. It was safer, I'm the skipper, he's the crew. Family understands and is more patient about good months and bad months.

I've never found it lonely at sea. It isn't only the workload is more than halved, many jobs take more than twice the time when done alone, but it's safer, you've got someone looking out for you.

We own a cafe overlooking the River Gannel, using a First Buyers Licence our shellfish comes into the cafe, and people come to eat in or takeaway. The rest of our catch goes to Hawkins at Hayle or Newlyn, we need both a premium and a wholesale route to market to be viable. We do wet fish too; monk, turbot, ray and pollock. I'm sure there's a future in fishing, you need to be adaptable and I'm planning a future without crew.

NEWQUAY RNLI
(L–R) Christian Brown and Mark Morris RNLI Helmsmen

"…for us, part of being in Newquay is always being involved in the sea…"

We have two Lifeboats: the first was a D Class with a crew of three and later an Atlantic 85 came with a crew of four, a slightly bigger boat. We usually take both boats, it extends our capabilities and rarely does any damage to have both boats out on a shout.

A lot of our shouts are to large groups, where having both boats means more space, many involve cliff falls so the easily manoeuvrable D Class gets in close to the shore for rescue, while the Atlantic 85 offers a more comfortable ride back for those who might be injured. The Atlantic is faster, but the D Class is agile, so we work both as a team.

The Helmsman chooses from the volunteers available and according to the type of job. If it's a cliff fall it's really nice to have a paramedic with you. We are RNLI Casualty Care trained but it's reassuring if someone can bring their day to day professional experience and skills to the task.

The BBC series Saving Lives at Sea showed us at work, it was very well received and we will be on it again.

JOE EMMETT
FISHERMAN - Phra-Nang

"…I'm just passionate about people getting out and eating more fish…"

We've just had two days off in thirty, every morning I get up, and look forward to going to work. Doing something I love and spending time with my nephew Sam. Much of my enjoyment in life comes from the way I make my living. If it doesn't work we just adapt to make it better.

Primarily we catch crab and lobster and some wet fish. We sell to Flying Fish at Indian Queens, it's easier that way, straight into the London market rather than storing it for the lorry to collect later. It's the modern way we've just adapted. Seafood has become more fashionable and is now almost too expensive as a day to day food.

Through a First Buyers Licence we sell direct to three restaurants within half a mile of the harbour. It's a win win, the fish hasn't gone through a middle man, so even with my mark up it's cheaper, they serve the freshest fish at a more affordable price, so more people can enjoy it.

I'm a keen gig rower and a Senior Helm with Newquay RNLI.

SAM HAMILTON
CREW - Phra-Nang

"…hopefully, as long as the industry is here I'll be in it…"

I finished school on a Thursday, by the following Monday I was working full time. I've had no real time off since, except when I broke my arm and couldn't work for a few months. I started with the Gilberts but we did a crew swap and I came to crew for my uncle, Joe Emmett.

In lessons at school I sat there thinking, I'm not going to need any of this as I'm going to be a fisherman and just catch fish. My dream would be to become a skipper one day either on my own boat or perhaps my Uncle's. For boats over ten metres there's an exam you have to do for a Skipper's Ticket.

I've been rowing for Newquay Rowing Club for twelve years now and came second in the County. I've not had the time to go to the World Gig Rowing Championships on the Scillies because I've been too busy fishing. I just love fishing and even when not at sea I like to fish for carp in the local fishing lakes, that's on a catch and release basis.

KEVIN 'MONKEY' ROGERS

"…it's so nice here, so relaxed, not like up country, no trouble, no stabbings, all we do with a knife is fillet a fish…"

I started with Dave Trebilcock years ago and helped him to find some flags in the fog, that was in the 1970's. I'm now the longest serving crewman down here on this harbour. I've been everywhere, to Ireland, all over. I was born in Newquay, went to Lowestoft to do trawling but that was boring so I came back here.

I started fundraising for Children's Hospice South West with running. Then I did Tough Mudder, it was hard, no one thought I could do it, they all thought I'd have a heart attack. It was a two and a half hour course near Penzance. I raised a very large sum and split it between the Mission and Cornwall Air Ambulance. The Fishermen's Mission always helps people down here, with the rent and so on, so why not give something back. We had a good do at the rowing club presenting the cheque.

I like it on Monday nights when I play Euchre at the Rowing Club, but I don't row or do the Lifeboat.

GARETH HORNER
OWNER - E RAWLE & Co FISHMONGER

"…we are one, in only a handful, of the oldest surviving businesses in the town…"

I've lived in Newquay all my life and come from a long established Newquay family. The business was established on this spot in 1936. Prior to that my Grandfather and his Brother in Law had separate businesses in the town.

We buy as much Newquay fish as possible, but there are items we have to buy from away. There have been quite a lot of changes recently, people have become more adventurous. They ask for different species especially since TV Chefs have campaigned for sustainable fish. The best example of this is pollock. Line caught pollock is one of the most sustainable fish species. There are other varieties like gurnard or dab which people wouldn't have heard about and now are more willing to try.

We've always prepared fish for our customers. These days people are more willing to get their hands dirty so take home a whole fish and play with it in the kitchen, there's so much knowledge out there now.

We do rely heavily on the holiday trade, we close in January for a break, my boys are living in Edinburgh and Manchester so no one in the family is coming on.

MARTIN AND DANIEL GILBERT

"...sun, sea, nice way of life, no interference, no noise, my own boss and even after forty years it's nice to see a dolphin looking around..."

Martin has two sons, Daniel and Jake. I'm proud of them both but they don't get on: so I've split them up and bought them a boat each. I don't come from a fishing family, I'm the first one. My grandfather was in the Royal Navy and my father a lorry driver. I came down to the harbour as a kid one summer holiday, went out on a mackerel trip and have been down here ever since. Born and bred in Newquay, never been anywhere else for long.

We fish for crab and lobster and in the winter use nets for pollock or cod; we travel anything from a hundred yards off the coast to twenty-five miles out. Most of it goes to Harvey's in Newlyn and then for processing. In the winter we do our maintenance, make pots, and sort out bait. The winters are hard. We sit tight.

Daniel: I left school and tried a career in refrigeration with an Uncle-in-Law in Bodmin. I'd always wanted to go fishing, I love it, the sea's in my blood so I'll always come back to it.

GARY EGLINTON

"…I used to sing with Chacewater Carnon Vale Male Voice Choir, it's quite a commitment and cost me too much fishing time, I still needed to make a living…"

My boat is The Shannon, owned by the family and we have two others. We fish for shellfish that goes to Spain, we've been selling to a reputable firm via an agent in Paignton for many years.
In the '70's we had the first Lamorna built by John Moor in Charlestown, there was a second Lamorna built in Mevagissey, both wooden boats. There's still a boat builder there, his son has taken over but I don't think they build many fishing boats anymore.

The SS40 is fibreglass and I built that boat from scratch. My father Ron, who will be ninety in August still goes out for mackerel, pollock and bass and a few pots in that boat. I've got two sons, one is skippering a wind turbine boat in the North Sea. My other son Ben has the Beryl M, which we bought last year from Belgium, it was built in Falmouth.

I did twenty-seven years on the Lifeboat and got a long-service medal from the RNLI at Buckingham Palace.

BEN EGLINTON

"…definitely a future, this is the time to get into the industry but boats need to be versatile and adaptable to all types of fishing, potting, netting and lining…"

I'm thirty-two born and bred in Newquay, never moved out. At seventeen I wanted to fish but my parents forced me into the Navy, telling me to go away and get a real job, earn a living, get a trade. Last year with the money I was given for fifteen years service, I bought a boat.

Dad's a boat builder by trade, having brought her back from Belgium, he and I spent twelve months and a lot of money refitting her. The sense of achievement was huge. She's called the Beryl M and we are all about looking after the catch, gaining a reputation for premium quality produce. As a result we get excellent prices.

Alongside we are developing Comfish Marine, supplying commercial fishing equipment and hoping to open a shop above the harbour.

My other half comes from a fishing background; I have two daughters, the youngest is slightly disabled and needs constant help. It takes a certain type of girl to go fishing but they come out with me.
Three dogs, including a puppy destined for the boat and I've done seventeen years for the RNLI.

RONALD ALFRED EGLINTON

"…I'm Cornish by two ferry chains, born on the front at Saltash into a family of Tamar salmon fishers, but my Father was in the building trade…"

I'm ninety, as a lad I looked out of my bedroom window where it says 'I K Brunel 1859' I thought he was my father until I was a bit older and I realised it was the milkman.

In the war I served in the Devon and Cornwall Light Infantry, ending up in 45th Royal Marine Commando based in Cyprus. I came back to Cornwall to work with my Dad and met a lady. We'd been married sixty-five years until she died last year: the Beryl M is named after her.

We had the Lamorna I and II, wooden boats built by John Moor in Charlestown. We couldn't have sold the Lamorna to a better family than the Pascoe family in Newlyn. I love to go down there and see her, she's as good as the day she was built. I think the world of them and value the lifetime of friendship greatly, we still see them regularly. Only last week Denys went to Scotland to pick up an award from Fishing News.

When you're in Newquay talking about the harbour, the fishermen, the rowing, the Lifeboat it's all the same gang, that's lovely, even still.

IAN JEPSON

"…the Chinese market wants to pay so much for crab local companies can't always get it. We've got to work that bit harder so we can look after and supply everybody…"

No, fishing isn't in the family. Dad was in the RAF, came from Scotland to Newquay forty-nine years ago, I was born here so I am Cornish. I was four when I started on boats. I left school in 1986 and have been fishing ever since, I worked for others for nine years and then bought my own boats, they are always called three Jays after my son.

I fish for crab and lobster and supply 'Seafood and Eat It' based in Newlyn, who have a contract with Waitrose to process and supply the crab.

My daughter lives with me, and my son with my ex-wife. I was a young helmsman with the RNLI here but had to resign when we got divorced as my little girl came first but I'd done twenty years with them, I really loved it and saved about 170 lives. My brother lives in London, it's great to visit but after the second day it's just awful, it's lovely by the coast.

DAVE TREBILCOCK

"…in the old days the social life of Newquay Rowing Club and the RNLI was quite different…"

I'm Newquay born and bred, Dad was a quality builder in the town. He said when you leave school you learn a trade, then you can go down the harbour fishing, so I never went fishing when I left school. I started as crew on a crabbing boat and progressed to a small boat of my own, lobster, crab, long lining for spurdogs.

I'm the longest serving member of Newquay RNLI, done twenty-eight and a half years in the crew and twenty-two as Deputy Launching Authority. The Lifeboat first came in 1965 and now we have two boats here, a D class and an Atlantic 85 mainly helping people in trouble on the beaches and cliffs.

RNLI old timers did a lot for us crew. Jack Parkyn a local farmer sold daffodils to raise funds and Les Hubbard a coach owner provided the transport for trips away to London, to thank us volunteers.

In 1981 Newquay Rowing Club was invited by the RNLI to represent the UK at the Independence Day Regatta on the Hudson in New York. We got to the final against the US Merchant Navy School, very fit muscular young men. Our boat including a couple of rowing old timers took the lead and won by half a length. We had a magnificent presentation at the New York Playboy Club and were presented with a trophy from the Emperor of Japan. A real highlight.

ADAM 'BUCK' BECKETT

"…My boat, Frellie is named after Freddie and Ellie my two children. PW40 was my Dad's boat registration, I just thought it would be nice to have it, so managed to find it…"…

We have had a very long winter, been out perhaps twenty five days in all of January, February and March and last year the run up to Christmas, November and December weren't too good either. We need to get some money in now, could well be doing twelve hour days seven days a week soon, let's hope so.

I've been fishing since I was fourteen and a half, I did a few years working away on super crabbers out of Newlyn and in Holland, but now own my own boat. I didn't do the RNLI as I just wanted to spend any spare time with my kids.

Freddie is fishing, fishing, fishing, but whereas I just disappeared from school he's got to stay on and finish. If he still wants to fish we can speed it up then by finding an apprenticeship or something. Ellie works in the restaurant over there, she doesn't want to go and I wouldn't want her to fish.
It's different these days.

PHILIP McKENNA
MARITIME ASSISTANT NEWQUAY HARBOUR

"…no really exciting happenings here, but mind, I've only been here a little while…"

Newquay Harbour is owned and run by Cornwall Council. I cover and deputise for the Harbour Master in his absence, his other port is St Ives. The role is as a point of contact for harbour users, be they fishermen, tripping boats, holiday makers or those who've come to launch vessels.

I ensure the health and safety of the harbour; inspecting safety equipment, making sure the railings, life buoys and rescue equipment are all fit for purpose and we monitor Channel 16 here too.

I've been associated with the harbour all my working life. First in the early 1980s as a fisherman, then between jobs on North Sea rigs and the fire service. I also worked as a commercial diver on 'civils' projects out of Falmouth: assessing repairs to shipping, insurance investigations, sunk vessels and at sea repairs to vessels that couldn't get in to dock.

I've always had two jobs: I'm also an Emergency Care Assistant with the Ambulance Service, I work in a team with a paramedic driving or looking after patients.

I don't have much time for hobbies or other things.

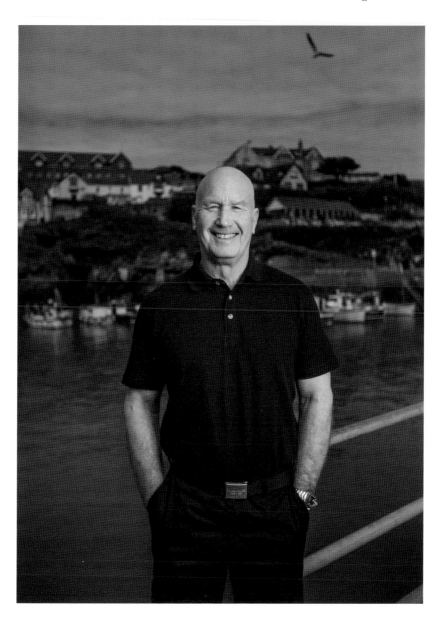

NEWQUAY HARBOUR MISSION

"…Newquay Lifeboat station is the only one in the world that has a Chapel as part of its structure…"

There's been some form of Christian mission on this spot since 1833. It has long served fishermen, initially providing 'improving' books and Christian literature. Later a wooden shelter was built and a Missioner employed. A Pleasant Sunday Afternoon (PSA) service was offered for fishermen in their working clothes.

The port was taken over by the local authority in 1929.
PSA continued but a declining congregation meant that the religious and pastoral care moved to a local Methodist Minister in 1982. A decade later the RNLI needed more space for bigger boats so the chapel was moved into the new building.

This opened in 1994 with the original wooden interior, pews, wall panels, floors, and decorations all restored inside. It is like time travel stepping inside. The Harbour Mission continues to open its doors offering refreshments and a welcome to visitors and locals alike.

The building is now used for various events during the year, including an annual Blessing of the Fleet Service led by the Fishermen's Mission. It provided a welcome seat and refreshing cup of tea for a number of the interviews in this section of the book.

THE BRODERICK FAMILY AND CATHERINE ANNE
(L–R) Junior Broderick, Danial Welsh, Robert Broderick and Shaunna Broderick

"…it made quite a difference having the Mission there…"

Robert is the owner of the Catherine Anne, he's been fishing for thirty-five years. He is now working with his two sons and occasionally his daughter.

They lost their Mother to cancer a year ago. She'd had the illness for three years and the Mission were really supportive. Keith helped me through a lot. I decided to stop fishing for a year and had to sell the boat we had in Newlyn. I was able to go back half fishing for a while and this year back fully.

Junior; I just want to fish, it's all I want to do and Danial has been crewing since he left school.

Shaunna volunteered for the RNLI crew at sixteen, she's now twenty-one. I'll crew for the Old Man when he needs it. I'm off to train up as a warfare specialist in the Navy. The RNLI encouraged me, I could either stay here and fish with my Dad or go and give back.

Dad is proud of her: following on at sea she'll get a good career out of it, spread her wings a bit, I'll miss her but won't miss the worry.

DAVID HARRIS

"...fishermen are versatile, especially in Cornwall. I have always had the greatest respect for them..."

I was MEP for Cornwall and Plymouth and then MP for St Ives from 1983 until I retired in 1997. Fishing was very important to me. It's funny how fate plays you a card; it played me one marked fish. I served on my party's Fisheries Committee in the House of Commons. I spoke in every fisheries debate during my years in the House and had close links with National Federation of Fishing Organisations.

I think one of my greatest contributions to the industry was in developing the Mackerel Box. Areas off the Cornish coast and in the eastern Celtic Sea where juvenile mackerel are protected by a ban on targeted fishing by some types of boats.

I always took an interest in fishing and felt a connection with the Fishermen's Mission. I always tried to visit relatives of anyone lost at sea, always going with 'the Mission man' particularly Len Scott. I was very honoured when they rang and asked if I would join the Council of Trustees. I joined after I retired and was Chairman between 2009 - 2012. I still keep in touch with the Mission, sometimes getting to their AGM with the chance to catch up with old friends. I'm always happy to shake a bucket and do my bit locally!

LIBBY SHAW AND ANDREW FORSTER
JOINT MANAGERS - WATERSTONES TRURO

"…we like to support local charities as much as we like to support local books…"

As a branch we've been fundraising for the Fishermen's Mission on and off since 2012, many of the staff are involved too. We did the Midnight Walk on Dartmoor a few years ago - it was a very long walk and we were the last back, it took us till 5 a.m!

We like to do joint ventures with other local businesses or community groups. Recently we've been working with The Great Cornish Food Store. Nathan Outlaw did the food for a Valentine's Evening, money from the ticket sales went to the Mission and we took pre-orders for Nathan's forthcoming book.

It is important to us that we support things that support the local community.

TRUSCOTT'S FISH AND CHIPS

"…I'm Diane with an e, there's nothing Princess like about me…"

The fish and chip shop has been here since 1969, my husband and I bought it off my parents in the 1980s. Our daughter worked with us for a while before going to work for the NHS and now my grand-daughter works with us. She might take it on one day, it's harder for family businesses now.
We close in December and January each year.

Laura, who works for us, lost her Dad at sea. Initially we didn't know he was lost, it took a good few days to find him. When Laura told us what the Mission had done for her and her sister I just thought what an excellent charity. They'd sent birthday and Christmas cards each year and kept in touch with her Mum making sure they were OK. Most charities help initially, then you get forgotten about.

The approach really appealed. We have Albert on the counter and sell fridge magnets for the Mission. A few years ago we were invited to London as a thank you. I'm a worker not a shirker and I liked their direct approach and their line, "Christianity with its sleeves rolled up."

PHIL 'LENS CAP' LOCKLEY
PHOTOGRAPHER FOR FISHING NEWS

"…without the fishing industry or the wonderful men and women that drive it, I'd probably be a retired teacher or a miserable git who never did what he truly wanted to do…"

My fishy life began at five years of age on holiday in Weymouth. I used a drop-net in Portland Harbour ending up with a feast of prawns, which I 'sold' to my parents for another source of pocket money. In1978 I moved to Cornwall to teach biology, but soon chose another job, bought a boat and began potting and netting and stayed for a few years.

Then in 1984 with nothing more than a notebook and camera I began to unravel the Westcountry fishing industry. All fishermen are square pegs in round holes and long may it continue!I visited almost every port, met many fishermen, recorded many boats, spent trips on some and found the best remedy for seasickness is plenty of cider afterwards.

Talking about and taking pictures of fishing and getting paid for doing it, is a life that many would dream of.

MARK HOLLEY
FUNDRAISER

"…Fish don't jump from the sea onto the plate, these men risk their lives to bring in the fish. I want to support them and their families when difficulties come…"

I'm seventy-three and in near perfect health. I've spent forty-four years in the UK, I'm an Anglo-Indian. I've got music in my blood, my father was into violins, organs and piano tuning, he'd be 105 now.

I'd always wanted to learn to play the sax. When I retired I bought a second hand Boosey & Hawkes 400. The shop showed me some technicalities but the rest I've taught myself. I can play over a thousand songs: jazz, blues, country, folk, love songs and rap. All you need is an ear for music, rhythm and to play from the heart, I can't read music, to me it's just doodling I can't understand.

I want to use the talents God has given me to benefit others. I've raised a lot of money for various charities over the years, playing in supermarkets and other places. When I saw what happened to Porthleven in the 2014 storms I got in touch with the Mission, Julian Waring saw my credentials so now I'm raising money for them.

JAKE AND RYAN GILBERT

"...any spare time gets spent in the pub..."

This is Dad's boat I skipper it. We fish for crab, lobster and shellfish. Shellfish seems quite sustainable. I used to play rugby for Newquay and I live two minutes away from the harbour. Ryan is my son.

My name is Ryan Martin Gilbert and I live in Trenance Road in Newquay. Daddy works on his boat. I like to come too. I have to go to school in ten minutes.

GEOFF AND CHRISTINE BROWN

"…one way and another we've been involved in saving lives at sea for twenty-five years or more…"

Geoff is Newquay born and bred. My current job is Cornwall Council Cabinet Member for Transport and I'm Chairman of the Harbours Board which manages all Council run harbours.
In 2014 my Council job was in Public Protection and when the storms hit I was in the Emergency Planning Centre watching as towns flooded and harbours were crushed. The Mission was there all the time, helping fishermen who hadn't been to sea for three months and were beyond the bread line.

In Newquay that year we held our first Blessing of the Fleet service in the Mission building, it has become an annual event. The Mission's pastoral work has now passed to a local minister but there is a welcoming team here most days of the year making drinks for fishermen and visitors alike.

Christine, is Geoff's wife. I'm Mum to seven, Grandmother to fifteen and a Great-Grandmother as well. I've been involved in Search & Rescue, Cliff Rescue and did seven years as an auxiliary watch in the Ops Room at Falmouth Coastguard, where our local knowledge was really valued. Shifts were three or four times a week, with some six hour night watches monitoring the distress frequencies.

JOHN AND VALENTINE TONKIN
FUNDRAISERS

John is from Newlyn but lives in Falmouth. All my family, going back many years have been Newlyn fishermen. The Royal National Mission to Deep Sea Fishermen is very important to my family. My Father collected for them and I've been collecting for them since about 1981. When Mr Scott was the Superintendent in Newlyn, he was very kind to Father, telling him when he retired he could have a small pension from the Mission. So for me it's time to give something back, to thank the Mission.

When I was a small boy the Mission was a very large building in Newlyn. We used to go in there to play dominoes, snooker or billiards if no fishermen were playing, however it was quite often frowned upon. We would go after school or in the evenings to have a chat and cup of tea. The Mission was always there and good for men who came in from abroad, especially on French or Belgian boats. They could have a bath and sometimes a bed for the night.

Valentine is John's wife. I did a little bit of House to House collecting for the Mission but mainly it was John's thing.

THE GREAT CORNISH FOOD STORE, TRURO

"…if people ask us for prawns or salmon we explain we don't have them as they don't come from Cornish waters: we always offer a genuinely local alternative though…"

Ruth Huxley is owner and managing director of the Store. Fish is one of the most popular counters in the Store, accounting for about ten percent of our turnover. It attracts a very high number of repeat customers. People are not aware of just how fantastic good fresh fish can taste.

Our fish comes daily from different parts of Cornwall particularly from the day-boats in Looe and shellfish brought in by Ian Jepson, who fishes from Newquay. We have oysters from Porthilly too. Both our fishmongers have degrees in marine subjects and are able to help customers with fish preparation or ideas for cooking, we really do want people to enjoy the local produce.

There is a cafe here as well where we offer a daily fish special. Paul Ripley who works for us, is a Stein trained chef who makes delicious soups, chowders and fish cakes as well as items for the deli counter. He too offers encouragement to those less sure about how to cook fish.

RUTH HUXLEY
OWNER - CORNWALL FOOD AND DRINK AND THE GREAT CORNISH FOOD STORE

"…when someone tells me something can't be done I'm even more determined to do it…"

Back in 2010 when I set up Cornwall Food and Drink there was no funding available to support food, drink and fishing businesses. We needed to think differently about how to develop and support these important sectors of the County's economy. Thinking strategically and commercially instead, the services we offered had to be right and of value so the industry would pay.

Cornwall Food & Drink was commissioned by the Local Enterprise Partnership and the Fisheries Local Action Group to identify opportunities for development in the fishing industry. Fishing wasn't seen, for some reason, as part of the food community. We had to get the message out to the consumer.
My knowledge of fishing improved and we published the Great Cornish Fish book.

Through this work I'd seen how important the Mission was to the industry. When I came to set up the fish counter at the Store I knew it had to have as much integrity as possible, including recognition of the hard and dangerous work fishermen did. Albert sits on the counter and a while ago we had Nathan Outlaw come to prepare a Valentine's Dinner, with proceeds going to the Mission.

SUE HENDRICKS AND FAMILY
(L–R) Jade, Ellie, Jenny, Sue and Sam
Brian

"…The Mission were there straight away and helped me to get through it all…"

I got involved with the Mission because eighteen years ago my husband died. Brian, 'Bommer' was a Newquay fisherman. As it was too rough to go out to sea that day, he went fishing on the rocks at Pentire and got washed away. I got a call from the Police, they came round to see me, they'd found a motorbike and all his fishing gear on the rocks. He was missing and found nine days later by other Newquay fishermen.

The children were still teenagers, Jenny was seventeen at the time and the Mission helped immediately with Tesco vouchers, someone to talk to and helped with the press, lots of things really.

Jenny has talked to the children about Brian. They know all about him, and what we've done with the Fish Wives Choir. It hasn't stopped them getting involved with the sea, we live near the sea and there are opportunities for them so it would be a shame to miss out.

The Mission haven't forgotten us, Julian still keeps in touch and involves us with all sorts of things.

BBC RADIO CORNWALL

BBC Radio Cornwall is part of the local radio family, made up of thirty-nine stations across the country.

With a place surrounded by water the sea features prominently in our day to day lives. Each morning we travel around ports and harbours keeping in touch with what is going on there – an important part of those contributions features fishing. It's not just the price of fish we are interested in, it's the safety onboard and the people involved in the businesses linked to one of Cornwall's traditional industries.

When families are more scattered we hope to provide company for the isolated and lonely, along with keeping the communities up to date with what's going around them. We offer programming, information, news and sport geared to local interests, as well as entertainment reflecting the best of Cornish communities.

We aim to bring people together – for large or small events – sharing those experiences with the whole of Cornwall and the Isles of Scilly. We want to stimulate debate and discussion about the things that really matter to our audience.

NEWQUAY COASTGUARD
(L–R) Dave Bulley, Leyton Bennett, Mat Relton

"…all the team are on call twenty-four hours a day, we drop everything and go where we are needed, very like the RNLI…"

Mat Relton is a member of the Newquay team. We are a team of fourteen, covering a thirty mile stretch of coast from Penhale Camp to Mawgan Porth. We all live in the area a few in Holywell Bay, a few in Mawgan Porth and five or six in town, the truck is at our base in Newquay. We are tasked to an incident by Falmouth Coastguard if necessary with the RNLI and the helicopters. During a shout the Coastguard co-ordinate the operation using Channel 0.

We come from various backgrounds: boats, police officers, hairdressers or mechanics. We train every Thursday, go on courses in Falmouth for first aid, rope rescue techniques and helicopter training. We can call on our colleagues in Padstow or St Agnes if we need to put two rope systems in place and on the RNLI for back up. They, of course, sit comfortably observing from their boats at sea while we work hard from the cliff top! We all have different roles but it's a great thing to work with all the others in a big team.

Padstow and Rock

THE McBURNIE FAMILY
(L–R) Amy McBurnie, Robert McBurnie, Sally McBurnie, Bruce McBurnie, Bonnie Connellan & Isaac,
L - R Donny McBurnie, Elizabeth

"…community, it's the people who make it special here…"

Robert's father came with the Scottish fishing fleet. I'd actively miss the bus to school, preferring to go fishing with my father. I've been married to Sally for thirty-six years, tried retiring a few years ago but now I've got a job on the car park.

Sally's been a fisherman's wife, not a fish-wife, for thirty-six years. Family is what matters most. All of us have been involved with the boats. Bruce has been as keen as anything, Rob tried to sneak off without him one day, I found him shouting at his Dad in the road to take him. This year he's going with Kevin Lance.

The girls loved going out with Dad but wouldn't touch the crabs or the bait. We'd stack the pots, but preferred swimming off the boat, hanging out at sea. It was a lovely childhood, swimming out to Dad off the beach as he waited for water to come in, we could get a lift back or go off to places you can only get to by boat.

Bonny is pleased not to have to go away to work. Working for Stein's means I'm employed all year, there are jobs and money around, the town doesn't just shut like it used to and I'm near my family.

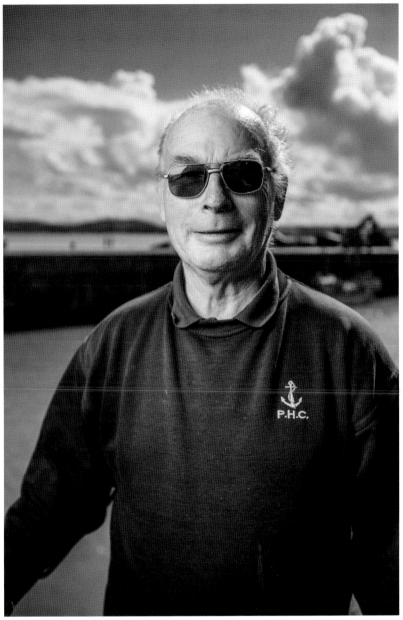

TIMOTHY JAMES NORFOLK
PADSTOW HARBOUR CARPARK

"…I don't go fishing or out to sea…"

My job is to pick up rubbish and empty the bins around the quay and look after the railings. I know most people and fishermen. Born here in Padstow. I was on the ferries to Rock for twenty-five years when they were ninety-two seaters in the 1970s and '80s. We used the ferry steps, not so much Health and Safety. It's a nice place, fairly busy and active with visitors in July and August.

I do a lot of collecting for the RNLI in the town. On Sunday last I did some egg rolling and raised nearly £100.00 for them. I go out to the Lifeboat station, make tea, and help with the launching and recovery of the Lifeboat. This summer there will be a two day collection out there so I might go to help with that, not decided yet.

I used to sing when I was younger when there was an accordionist at The London Inn on Saturday nights, that was a lot of fun.

TEAM PRAWN ON THE LAWN
RICK AND KATIE TOOGOOD

"…if it swims or lives in the sea, we get it, sell it and cook it…"

Rick grew up in London and came to Rock in the summers. Katie is from Taunton not too far from the sea. We just wanted to open something together for the future. Prawn on the Lawn started in London as a fishmongers with a difference. Johnny Murt supplied us in London and then encouraged us to open in Padstow, he and his brother still supply us with fish.

Before we knew it our fishmongers was turning into a restaurant, customers came to eat small tapas style plates, or choose their fish from the counter for us to cook as they'd like, classic, Thai or Chinese, rather than buy the fish to take home.

It's a very creative way to work: our whole menu is based on whatever the fishermen bring in, we don't know from one day to the next what the catch will be. This means locals and visitors can come regularly and find something new and exciting.

We are about to open a new restaurant up the road, Barnaby's, the offerings there will change once a month or so and include locally reared meat.

MATTHEW 'CHINGEY' CHOWN

"…more chance of the girls going fishing actually, they are keen and willing, my boys are more interested in football…"

This is the seventh generation of fishermen in my family. Two from Padstow, the rest from Plymouth all fishing and naval families. I do lobster and line caught bass. Occasionally I go out with my brother, on the Harvest Reaper trawling from Newlyn for a week or so if someone wants a break. We target rays, soles and plaice which go direct to Ocean Fish, they pay us according to market averages at Newlyn and Plymouth - the fish ends up either locally or across the UK.

I've three daughters and two sons, it would be a first in my family to have the girls come on, it would be lovely. They are a bit young so we go out on the river, this year we'll start with rod and line. There are a few women in fishing on the south coast. Elizabeth Stevenson in Newlyn has pushed hard and done well in the business, I wouldn't dissuade them at all, there's a good future and if they want to do it they can.

THE TEAM AT STEIN'S

Rick and Jill Stein opened The Seafood Restaurant in Padstow back in 1975. From humble beginnings the business now employs over six hundred staff and includes twelve restaurants, forty hotel rooms, self-catering accommodation, four shops and a cookery school. The business has grown beyond Cornwall with restaurants in Winchester, Sandbanks, Marlborough and London. These days, forty years on, their three sons are all involved in the business, keeping the family very much involved with the strong management team who run the day to day operation. Everyone in the organisation knows that working as a fisherman is a dangerous and lonely job. The have always done what they can to help The Fishermen's Mission.

GAVIN WICKS
Emma Kate II

"…Gav's shy, he likes being out on his own…"

I'm here mending a rat hole in my pots, and I ain't good at talking which is why I hid from you yesterday.

I'm from a fishing family, my Dad's retired now but he's still got a boat, my brother, he's got a tripping boat called Emma Kate. I grew up here and live in Trevone.

BRONCO'S FAMILY
(L–R) Sophie Harding-Reeks, Haley Harding-Taylor, Kelly Harding,
(L - R) Roxy Harding-Reeks, Carley Benson
Bronco

"…When Nan had The Harbour Inn she wanted to write a book and call it "Harbour These Memories", we would like to harbour these memories…"

Haley was married to Neil Harding but he preferred to be called Bronco. This is hard to say really: my husband has been gone twenty six years this year. To me I still remember as if it were yesterday and will always think like that. Fishing was his life, he did love it. He was a well known man, a big softy, a proud family man who thought the world of his daughters. I just look at my daughters and see Bronco in them every day. He'd have been proud of being a Grandad, he loved his close-knit family.

We'd have liked to go fishing with him, but were too young - he always said he'd take us out to see the dolphins but unfortunately that never happened. He'd have liked to put us in a nunnery but that never happened either! I hate fishing because it took my Dad away and I wouldn't want my son to go fishing. You can't put into words how you feel. In some ways it's easier for me because I didn't really know him but now I'd like to ask him "what would you do Dad?".

The Fishermen's Mission helped us and that's why it's so close to our hearts, they were there for us. They helped and visited Mum when she lost Dad, helped with putting a fund away for us. We had fantastic support from the Padstow community.

JOHNNY MURT

"…I went away to the USA, got a degree in Marine Biology, a Masters in Fishery Conservation Biology, a wife, an ex-wife - a good experience all round…"

I'm part of a Padstow fishing dynasty. My Dad and an uncle fished together for forty years and finished three years ago. Things have changed dramatically since: the Chinese market is breathing life into the crab industry. It used to be a mass production process; now it's also a sustainable, top quality product with a face on it and a premium price tag.

Through email contact with Rick and Katie Toogood I sent produce to Prawn on the Lawn in London. Rick's family had holidays in Rock so when a restaurant came up here I told him to buy it and he did. I take my produce to Prawn on the Lawn, a short walk across the quay, children and holiday makers in the town see this, they can ask questions and I can explain where the food comes from: transparent, just in, low food miles, top quality and sustainable.

I get to sell more fish, we get to have beers together.

MARTIN MURT

"…I love fishing, it's a family tradition, I've bought my own boat recently, it's my peace…"

Born and bred in Padstow I was fishing crab and lobster from 1991 - 2003, now I'm a whole time fire-fighter here and in Newquay. A while ago I restarted fishing but this time wet fish, mackerel and sustainable line caught species. A smaller amount of prime quality fish sells for a higher price.

Over the past five or six years I've built up relationships with the chefs here and in Rock. There is a market for prime fish from day boats. When I go to the restaurants the fish is still flipping, less than two hours old and people are prepared to pay for that. Excess goes to market via Ocean Fish or Flying Fish, the smaller specialist fishmongers involved in the day boat trade.

I've got two young sons, but I'd rather they found work which was more regular, and use this as a productive pastime. I guess I'm biased but I love it here and yes the tourists make it busy, but that's the price you pay for living in a stunning place.

KEVIN LANCE AND LAUREN PAYTON
OWNER - GOLDEN MASTER & NORTHERN LIGHTS

"…it's so easy to enjoy what's here, five minutes to beaches or out on the moors with the dogs…"

Kevin has been fishing since he left school. I started in Newquay for other people. When I got my own boat I came to Padstow, there was no space for any new boats in Newquay, it's a small harbour and there's more space here. It's about a thirty minute drive.

These days I have two boats with two skippers and I do most of the shore work, mending gear and looking after the boats. When I do go to sea Lauren will come with me. The boats go out every day for crab, we do a little bit of lobster early in the season but mainly crab. It's two and a half miles down the river to the sea and then we go anything from six to twenty miles out.
We use echo sounders to work out where the softer ground is.

I've just taken up gig rowing again in Newquay, I used to do it when I was younger.

Lauren came from Nottingham to chef for Rick Stein. Coming from the city furthest from the coast in the UK this is a forever destination. I came alone, I feel welcome everywhere. I'm now working at a place in Newquay, it's a little more chilled and I love it here. I like the boats too. Lance's family live nearby in Newquay so it's fine.

JASON NICHOLAS
Levan Mor

"…can't help but go through Padstow and see something to be proud of, coming from here, Padstow's a special place, we call it a proper place…"

We are out daily from five in the morning till six or later in the evening, depends on tide and weather. We supply lobster and spider crabs to Spain, Stein's with lobster and jet crabs. It is seasonal and this has been a long winter, the water is still very cold (mid-April).

We pick and process a lot of our own crab in a little unit, distributing to local restaurants and outlets. It gets as far as London: in 2016 we supplied Wimbledon and Queen's tennis competitions. All our business comes through word of mouth, it's a lovely product.

So many old fishing communities have died out, here we have May Day which helps keep our community traditions. Family is important, boats are often owned and crewed in families it's a whole ethos, anyone who comes out on a boat with you needs to buy into that aspect.

In seventeen or eighteen years time I'd be proud to have a nice business and a sustainable fishery for my boy to have.

SCOTT CHAPMAN
CREW - Levan Mor

"…I've just moved into Padstow from five miles away, it's worth an extra ten minutes in bed every morning…"

I've lived five miles away all my life and hoping to stay in this industry. My girlfriend and I went to New Zealand for three months, hired a camper van and travelled around. We saw a very interesting cray fishery in the South Island. As well as different ways of regulating fishing.

I've not got any children, well, none that I know of! Sadly I can't serve on the Lifeboat as I have colour vision disability which prevents me passing the medical. I do gig rowing though, in the Padstow Men's A Crew, done that for about eleven years now, we're off to the Scillies for the Gig Rowing World Championships soon.

DAVID EVANS

"...it's hard work, fishing, but it's the only place I get any peace..."

This boat is the first 19' 8" Shamrock Buccaneer, built in Camborne in about 2002, bought from a chap in Falmouth but it's registered in Truro. It's mainly for crab and lobster but there's a little trawl on it for flat bottom feeding fish, haddock, whiting, soles and monks. Most of it goes to Mr Stein or I take it home and eat it.

My sister and I have a residential lettings business but it means more to me going out in a boat than any of that. I've always fished: side trawling with Stevensons out of Newlyn with a Padstow crew, then with a skipper's ticket to Brixham and boats of my own. These days, forty-six years later, I just like playing around in a boat.

I'm a Deputy Launching Authority for the Padstow Lifeboat. I used to be on the crew when Trevor England was Coxswain but when he died I stopped that.

BRIAN BATE

"…it's a hard business, it's hard work, but the rewards are good sometimes - it's alright…"

I've been fishing out of Padstow since I was a young lad and now Captain of this fine ship, she's new to me. She'll be catching crab and lobster, anywhere between two and fifty miles off-shore. At the moment most of it goes to Scotland for processing: whoever pays the highest price!

Fishing was taking up more and more time so about ten years ago I stopped being on the Lifeboat crew but I'd done about fifteen years with them.

My son is coming on into fishing, he's now skipper of my ex-boat Northern Lights out of here too.

JACK GLAVES   ROBERT CHAPMAN

JACK GLAVES

"…it's a hard life, a real life, but I don't want to go anywhere else…"

I've been in the Merchant Navy for five years, now a 3rd Officer; before that I was fishing out of Padstow and Newquay. Fishing was very slack at the time and I needed money so joined the Merchant Navy. I did three years training as a cadet at Fleetwood Nautical College working on tankers and PG Tankers. The job's been great, I've travelled, seen the world and it's been very interesting.

Padstow is my family home and has been for generations, Father, Grandfather and Great-Grandfather were either fishing, in the Royal Navy or Merchant Navy. It's a long way back but it's where I like to come home to every time. I do three months out and three months home, when I'm here I see my friends and help them out, do a bit of work on the Mannin dredger here and just enjoy life. It's full of lively characters and it's the best community.

ROBERT CHAPMAN

"…Jack's Grandad used to fish with my Grandad and we are great friends now…"

In the summer I work on the Jubilee Queen and in winter do commercial fishing on the Kelly Marie. The Jubilee Queen is a domestic passenger vessel which takes people out on wildlife tours during the season, usually from Easter till the end of September. Going north towards Lundy Bay and Moles Island, we usually see dolphins, seals, puffins, guillemots and razor bills, it's about an hour and a half trip. I drive the boat, sit on top out of the way while the crew do the rest! The boat has recently been refurbished so we can do evenings with a full bar.

In the winter we fish for pollock on the wrecks, with crew, four days at sea, come back, land, get ice, fuel and food and go back again as long as the tides are right.

I've been on the Rock Lifeboat since I was eighteen, that's a great thing to do. I worked in the boatyard over there too for a while. Padstow, Polzeath where I lived as a child and Rock, just lovely places to be.

BERNARD MURT

"…don't know any different really, it's just lovely…"

Autumn Rose is the name of my boat and it does crab and lobster.
I'm born and bred in Padstow, from a large fishing family, my two older brothers are fishermen,
my nephews Johnny and Martin are also fishing from here. My son Thomas has been down
Newlyn fishing for the last four or five years netting and has made enough money to buy his own
boat, hopefully out of Padstow now.

I used to be on the Lifeboat.

TOM MURT

"…doing the same as my family do…"

My father, uncles, cousins are all fishermen, I come from a big fishing
family: grandfather died last summer. I've been down Newlyn working on
some bigger boats for four years now. Just bought my own boat and
starting alone in Padstow later this year. It'll be crabs, lobster that sort of
thing. I live in St Issey a few miles away.

It's just home.

KAREN PORTER

"…when he comes in, on the first night I let him snore, after that I'm not putting up with it…"

I've been married to Simon Porter (Partner/Skipper Karen of Ladram) for twenty-three years. It's a very very lonely life, I married into it so I knew I'd have to put up with it. I didn't plan to marry into fishing, we are both Padstow born and bred, lots of local family.

We have three children, Jamie, Larissa and Kelly. Kelly went on a trip with him a few weeks ago, I wasn't worried. I did keep ringing to make sure she was alright, she got a little sea sick but got through it and she'd probably go again. When the children were small and Simon was in he was very very good, took over completely, did the night feeds, looked after me. It is lonely, I miss him more now the children are gone. I've got a bit depressed recently.

I lost my Dad five years ago, I'd nursed him, you just need someone around then, with Simon at sea that was hard. When Dad died Simon came back in. Simon's given me a very good life, I don't want for anything. Now he's putting one of the crew through the skipper's training we'll be able to go away a bit together: perhaps Jamaica in January!

SIMON PORTER

"…I didn't see much of my children when they were young, but you've got to provide for your family…"

Simon is on the left. I'm the skipper/owner of the gill-netter Karen of Ladram, fishing for hake, monk and turbot out of Newlyn, she's too big to get out of Padstow. We spend a lot of time at sea, probably three weeks in the month, twelve months of the year. If you want to go to sea and put the effort in you'll do alright, nothing's gifted to you.

A Newlyn mate of mine started using Twitter, we use it to keep in touch with our chefs and buyers, they see the fish being caught, it goes down well with the customers. My daughter is a waitress near here, if someone orders the fish she says "my Dad caught that fish, here's a picture". She did a trip with us this winter; that was a big story. I needed crew, she offered, it's not often we have women with us, it worked well.

I'm in the wheelhouse by myself all the time it's a solitary job; responsible for the crew down on the deck together laughing and joking. You're in charge of their safety taking decisions that earn them a living too. It can be very solitary.

SIMON 'SID' PORTER

"…we've had a lot of tragedies over the years in Padstow, we've lost a lot of young men…"

Sid is on the right. I spent nearly all my working life at sea, fishing, Royal Navy or Merchant Navy. In 1992 I went to work on the stand-by boats in the North Sea and stayed there till I retired three years ago: it was alright, month on, month off and the money wasn't bad.

In 2016 I was elected Chief Officer for the North Cornwall Royal Antediluvian Order of Buffaloes (Buffs). The Fishermen's Mission was my nominated charity for my year in office, we raised just shy of £8,000 that year. We held various events but one of the best things was to offer Boxes of Fresh Fish as prizes, from my two sons who were skippers. It was brilliant way of raising money.

The Mission is well known in Padstow I don't suppose there are many Padstow families, born and bred here, that haven't had a bereavement of a father, son, brother or cousin - we've all been touched.

ED 'THE BASS' SCHLIFFKE - OWNER PADSTOW ANGLING CENTRE
(L–R) Duncan Randall, Bryan Robinson, Ed Schliffke

"…I was the first professional shore fishing guide in the country…"

I came to Padstow on holiday to a caravan at Treyarnon aged six or seven. I fell in love with rock pooling and the sea and have loved fishing ever since. I'm an engineer by trade but that hunter gatherer thing was so strong I'm following the dream.

I've been an angling guide, for bass and mackerel for thirty five years; teaching and guiding rod and line angling from rocks or beaches or my boat Rockhopper. It's a bit seasonal, we've had an awful winter this year. The species come in at different times of year; in winter there will be whiting and haddock, in summer mackerel, and pollock most of the year. Today we've been out on Rockhopper, twelve miles off, fishing reefs and wrecks for the pollock.

When I first started I'd have groups of two to twelve kids come out, but not now. They are not fishing any more, the electronic age has taken over big time and parents see fishing as too risky. We have many returning older holidaymakers who still want to learn so I must be doing something right.

ROBERT 'FLEA' THOMPSON

"…I've got two young sons, but I'm not going to recommend fishing to them, I'll be the last of the line…"

I'm passionate about fish which is why I'm working for Rick Stein as a fishmonger, been doing that for about four years now. I'm a third-generation fisherman, following my Father and Grandfather who was killed mine-sweeping in 1939. Done thirty-two years since I left school on the River Camel. Shellfish, crab and salmon fishing and a keen angler for sea bass.

Dad gave up fishing when he was sixty-two then I had the salmon licence for the River from him. Salmon fishing was stopped here in 2017 for ten years as the stock levels were critical. We used to go out in the day and night depending on tide conditions. I stopped going in daylight because other activities on the river made it too risky with the nets. So now it's anglers only now on catch and release.

I have a small commercial boat for my days off or after work, catching mackerel and bass and I love living here.

BEN EVANS & AMY O'NEILL
BEN'S CRIB BOX CAFE

"…I've not seen or heard anything…"

There's been a café on the harbour for generations. 'Ben's Crib Box', does breakfast for those working in fishing, the lorry drivers and those in the boatyard, anyone on the harbour really.

I came to Padstow aged four, twenty-eight years ago and took over the café from Jeff nine years ago. We serve 'breakfast' from 8 till 2.30 every day of the year. 'Full Cornish' in any combination, cooked to order and served at one of six tables. I do takeaway too, fresh bread, Breakfast Baps, tea, coffee, a short list of smoothies and cold drinks. On Monday and Tuesdays there are paninis.

Amy is Ben's partner and a local photographer: I'm sure he could have written a book full of what goes on, there's not much he doesn't know about.

It's lovely people feel they can come alone, old chaps whose daily highlight is a wander round the harbour come in for refreshment and company. Fishermen's children are brought to have crib with Dad when he's in. Hopefully those young ones will still be coming as young adults and still having crib here when they join the harbour workforce in years to come, we are part of the Padstow community.

CREW OF THE PADSTOW LIFEBOAT

"…you never know what's happening when the pager goes off, that keeps it so interesting…"

Mike England is Second Coxswain/Mechanic of the Padstow Lifeboat. A Tamar Class slipway launched boat, sixteen metres long, she's been here since 2006. We have twenty-eight crew, including the inshore crew. The Coxswain and myself always go on a shout taking five or six volunteer crew. It's a snap decision who goes depending the on weather and what the job is: first-aid, towing, mechanical or engineering, or searching. Everyone brings different skills but a shared attitude of dedication.

We've seen some harsh shouts: saving all the crew when a boat is destroyed is satisfying but helping out at tragic events is also part of the job. It's interesting, each day is different. We have a number of long standing crew, our head winchman joined in 1967, he's just got an extension to stay on, our Coxswain has done thirty five years. My first shout was when I was fifteen and my Dad was Coxswain: many families have provided Lifeboatmen for generations. We have builders, carpenters, a plumber, harbour staff, a stone floor repairer, a cleaner, a student nurse, two merchant seamen and of course fishermen.
A little bit of Padstow in St Merryn Parish.

'BIG BERNARD' SMALE

"…it's a lovely community here, special, been here all my life…"

In 1989 my life was saved from a trawler sinking when I was injured, I continued to fish but in 1994 I was injured again and had crushed shoulders. Although I went fishing again it was too much for my shoulders. I had to have two operations: there was nothing more they could do for me so I had to give up fishing. Sad.

Now I'm in the Chough Bakery working which is fine.

IVAN AND REGGIE BATE

"…it's getting harder, it's a good fishery and we've had twelve good years…"

Ivan's been fishing in Padstow all his life. Now I've got two boats one for lobster and crab, the other for monk and turbot, that one is about seventy miles down off the Scillies, the season has just started same as the lobsters.

We've had good times and bad times, we can't afford to change, fishermen can't afford to buy fish any longer, it's only for the wealthy now. We land in Appledore, North Devon and to Camel Fish at Rock. Most of our lobster go to Billingsgate. Crabs are packed in straw and ice boxed then flown to China, the price at the moment is the best we've ever seen.

Reggie is coming on behind Ivan now. I've been fishing since I was two and now just taking over the skippering. I am worried it's all going to fall apart with so many political changes but we shall see.

TIM AND LISA TUTTON
FORMERLY OF THE LONDON INN

"…we'll continue to support The Mission, it's just part of our life…"

Tim's been at sea for a total of twenty two years. We've been supporters of the Fishermen's Mission for ages. Both our families lost men in the two accidents in 1992, the Mission did a lot for us then. It's a good charity, big in our community.

We've done all sorts to raise funds for the Mission. Had T-Shirts and hoodies printed, fish feast nights around Christmas and raised over £2,000 in thirteen hours at our Tattoo Festival. The children all grew up with Gina, the previous Mission fundraiser as part of their lives.

I'm also the Fishermen's Mission Honorary Agent in Padstow, its a voluntary job. Most weeks I'm down on the quay chatting to the boys seeing if there's anything to help with. When the Brixham boys are in with trawlers in January I'll often drive them up to Tesco to help get the food in. We have a chat in the car about all sorts really. Sometimes if they're short of crew they ask if I could go to sea, I'm not doing that now, but I do miss it.

WALTER 'WALLY' CHOWN

"…things changed when we moved from wooden to steel and plastic pots, the crayfish wouldn't go anywhere near the plastic pots, but lobsters are OK…"

My whole life has been around the quay here. I started with David Chapman in 1968 or so with wooden pots, no long lining, I've been shellfishing always. We used to go to the Scillies in the Spring of the year with the Newlyn crabbers, Harveys and Rowses for crayfish. I've owned various boats over time, the first one I bought in 1977, from Phil Trebilcock in Newquay. Later I bought Lady be Good from Donny McBurnie. I left a boat to one of my nephews in Daymer. I live here in Padstow and have three nephews fishing out of Newlyn but my boy didn't follow me, he's a school teacher in Mevagissey.

I've been a Harbour Commissioner for twelve years now, we are responsible for running the quay with the Harbour Master, dealing with things like railings and other health and safety matters, as well as making sure the sand is kept out of the channel.

PADSTOW SEA SAND Co.
(L–R) Matt Prynn, Chris Prynn, Alan Boylan, Jack Prynn

"…nobody knows more about dredging than the Dutch, their whole country is built out of the sea…"

Chris Prynn works for Padstow Sea Sand Co. We dry excavate sand where instructed by the Harbour Commissioners to keep a main channel open for boats. We land the sand, take it to our yard, screen it to remove impurities before selling it on to farmers as a soil improver. It's also used by sand schools for horses as it's very soft sand. The customer can choose: to collect from here or we deliver anywhere from Land's End to Bridgewater in Somerset including North Devon.

It's a constant task depending on weather. Wind and storms bring the sand into the river; sometimes it's faster to fill than others but a NW wind fills it up the quickest. I learned about dredging in Holland, came back to Padstow and encouraged the Commissioners to do something similar with dredging here.

People spend thousands of pounds to come here for a week of holiday; I can earn my living here and I don't intend to retire. Being involved with both fishing and farming what better way could there be to fulfil your life as a Cornishman.

CHARLIE LUKE
PADSTOW HARBOUR PART-TIME CAR PARK ATTENDANT

"…I used to love it when the old steam trawlers were here…"

The people I meet are lovely, some have been coming here for sixty years,
they brought their kids and now those kids are bringing their kids.
I'm a young eighty-five and have seen a lot.

There was a time when the harbour was full enough you could walk all the
way across on boats, but these days there's hardly any left, fishing is dying
out slowly.

With this view you don't need to go away. I've got everything I could want
here and there is nothing wrong with the weather, you've just got to dress
up for it.

And by the way that'll cost you a quid!

PADSTOW BOATYARD

"…I am not a business man but a boat builder so I carry on doing what I do best…"

Will Claxton, fifth from the left, owner of Padstow Boatyard. We build new fishing vessels specialising in fibreglass, aiming for the twelve to fifteen metre end of the fleet. We have a one hundred and fifty tonne refit facility. Offering an almost unique slipway service and getting the boats inside so it's not weather dependent. This attracts commercial customers from Ireland, Brixham and even further; they want a job done and turned round as fast as possible so they can get back to work.

Originally I'm from Falmouth, went into the Marines and after five years set up a mobile boat building business all over the world using more exotic composite materials. Four years ago needing to settle as the children were getting older, we bought this business. It's grown a lot very fast, so recently we've employed someone to develop and expand the business in a sustainable way.

There's a boat around the back my eight year old built, she's a bit young yet, I don't want to get done!

SEASALT PADSTOW

From as far back as 2012, Seasalt has championed the Fishermen's Mission, in supporting the lives of fishermen and their families. From night-time trekking over the wilds of Dartmoor to charity bake sales, Seasalt is thoroughly committed to the Charity's aims of practical welfare and emergency support.

To date they have raised an incredible £77,700 and for every £1 donated 88p goes to active and retired fishermen and their families.

Speaking about the relationship and Seasalt's fundraising contribution, co-founder and chairman Neil Chadwick says: "We've always had a close affinity with the Fishermen's Mission. Many of our shops are in towns with strong fishing communities and traditions. We're pleased to have been able to raise their profile and we're delighted to have raised such a significant amount for them over the last six years."

PADSTOW HARBOUR OFFICE STAFF

"…there's lots of tea made and drunk…"

The Harbour Office is at the centre of the harbour over looking the comings and goings.
The Harbour Master is in charge here.

There's lots of administration, anything to do with keeping the harbour running. Invoicing, payroll, port administration, chasing debtors, sorting out any new legislation requirements such as GDPR or consultations on the new Marine Conservation Zones. Reception is here, helping visiting sailors, answering questions and a bit of a tourist information centre at the moment.

The Berthing Masters use this as their base, they are here two hours either side of every high water, every single day of the year except Christmas. They open the tidal gate and let in all vessels that need to stay afloat and offer advice on moorings etc. We organise fuel for leisure and commercial boats and ice for fishermen. The Shore staff are based here too, they do anything from fabricating ladders to picking up litter.

All the administration associated with the Car Park and the Rock Ferry is also done here. We are lucky to have a wonderful staff, four of them have done in excess of twenty five years service each.

WAYNE 'FOSSET' GAMBLE
PADSTOW SOCIAL CLUB

"…behind the bar in the Social Club looking around I know everyone, you can't do that down town these days…"

I live in the house I was born in, it was at the top of the town then. Now they've built and built and I'm in the middle, with a view looking right down the river.
I have a little fifteen foot punt I play about in, bassing. I used to do salmon but that's been stopped now. I was a Padstow fisherman for twenty-eight years before I had a bit of an accident and I've not been back to sea since. Now I'm working at Padstow Social Club, barman and doing a bit of maintenance.

After my accident the Fishermen's Mission helped, Julian and Keith looked after me. I'd been struggling to claim benefits and after fourteen weeks had no money. I got very flustered. They came up and put me in touch with SAIL, the Seaman's Advice and Information Line. I phoned at 10 am the next day and money was in the bank by 2pm. It really helped.

I've raised funds for them with the Buff Lodge and we always have the Alberts on the bar.

NICK 'SLOPE' CHAPMAN

"…fished everywhere, as far north as the Isle of Man, south as far as the top of Biscay, as far east as the Channel Islands and west as far as the Continental Shelf…"

I was twelve or thirteen when I started fishing, had my first boat at seventeen, worked for my father, been a skipper of the Harvest Reaper and other boats, Pilot Star and Pathfinder and more. We've done everything, gill-netting, long lining, everything. I like gill-netting the best as it's selective and there's little waste. I've got one of my sons on with me. We've landed fish all over, Newlyn, Roscoff, Ireland, Holyhead and Brixham and we use a Bideford company called T & T Fish.

My success has been down to having some of the best crews in the South West, men who have worked for me have gone on to be top skippers in bigger boats in Newlyn. I've always loved Padstow, everything is set up for us here, it's still home.

I don't want to be in the big league now, too old, that's a job for a younger man. I still enjoy what I'm doing now, two or three days is fine.

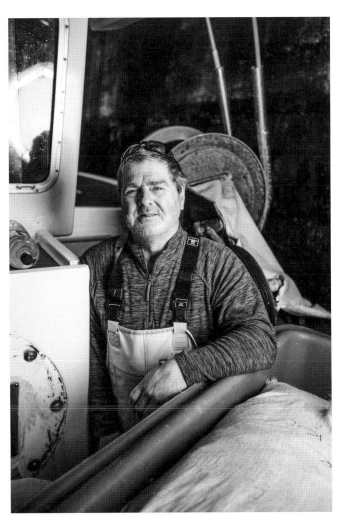

SPEED BOAT DRIVERS ON THE CAMEL RIVER
(L–R) Alan Hoskin, Peter O'Neill, Jack O'Neill, David Lockwood

Alan's Granfer started fishing out of Lowestoft on trawlers, his father was a Padstow trawler-man. When Alan left school he thought it looked a bit of a hard life; so now takes visitors out on Fireball his speed boat, he's also a Harbour Commissioner.

David Lockwood carries passengers around the Camel Estuary for a living, he's been in Padstow a while now, well, forty-seven years, loves the fishermen too.

Jack, Peter's grandson, can be heard on the quay calling attention to the speed boat services at weekends and in school holidays. He'd love to live in Padstow but makes do with Wadebridge just down the river, where he goes to school. He definitely wants to be a speed boat driver when he grows up, maybe fishing but he wouldn't want to live anywhere else.

Peter O'Neill has been involved in the fishing industry since leaving school, a buyer at Newlyn Fish Market, a vivier truck driver taking live shellfish around Europe for twelve years and now a recently elected Harbour Commissioner in Padstow - taking visitors around the Camel Estuary.

MIKE ENGLAND

"…I'm going to be here forever…"

I get a lot out of Padstow so like to put a lot back. Four generations of my family have lived in the same house in Church Lane and been fishermen and lifeboatmen in Padstow. Before I was born, Mum went fishing with Dad, they'd haul pots perhaps two or three times a day. Mum also made toys for a local gift shop and Dad was a shipwright too, they made ends meet.

I was never going to go fishing: thought about university, but spent a summer fishing with Dad and that was it. I was twenty-three when Dad died, I took on the family fishing business so education faded from view. Working for the Lifeboat is fairly solitary but I'm happy in my own company.
I'm a Harbour Commissioner too: I like poking my nose into other people's business.

Padstow has a uniqueness and maintains its community spirit: May Day especially. Padstow Carollers is important to me though. There's a strong tradition of carols in Cornwall, brought from port to port by fishermen. We sing unaccompanied four part harmonies around the town during Advent and on Christmas Eve in the main hall at Prideaux Place. It's important to keep these traditions alive so the community remains strong.

GLENN CHAPMAN AND DANIEL WILLIAMS

MARTIN AND KIRSTY MASTERS
DAVID MASTERS

" …When tragedy strikes it's tough, to lose five men in one week, we all pulled together, that's to be preserved and strengthened for the future…"

Martin has lived in Padstow all his life. I've got my own business lorry driving, don't want to move but I don't like it when it's so busy. My work is nothing to do with fishing, I never liked it, I'll leave it to others. I deliver aggregates and sea sand from Padstow to all around Cornwall, I will go to Devon but I just like Cornwall.

My brother was a fisherman, he drowned in 1992 on a fishing boat coming in from crabbing on a Sunday. He loved his fishing, he was out with his cousin and a good friend. We have never found his body which is very sad. So sad.

When we lost my brother, Kirsty's Uncle, the Fishermen's Mission were good to us. Mr Scott came up every week to help Mum and Dad. I'm very proud of Kirsty doing this sponsored running to raise more funds for the Mission.

****

Martin should also be proud of his daughter for the time and work she put in for this book in Padstow. Using all sorts of methods to get reluctant fishermen and others to participate, our little team could not have achieved this book without her. Endless, chasing and cajoling, explaining complex family trees to me, not to mention her amazing talent for briefing me in two words and a look. I loved our days together in Padstow and the Fishermen's Mission says thank you too. DR

ROB ATKINSON
PADSTOW HARBOUR MASTER

"…my favourite duty is going out on boats, least favourite is the paperwork; unfortunately going out on boats is getting less less and paperwork more and more…"

I've been Harbour Master here for eleven years, it's my job to keep order around the harbour. In winter we do maintenance work so in the summer when the place is packed with leisure craft and people there are very few 'works' to do.

I'm a pilot for the River so need to keep my knowledge of the harbour up to date, it has strong cross currents and sand banks means getting caught out is easy. I go out on the dredger for practice. We don't get many big boats in here, occasionally the Balmoral comes in from Lundy but mostly it's fishing and leisure craft.

I live near Penzance, with my wife Jo and three sons, Dan, Matt and Jon. I was on the Penlee Lifeboat crew for ten years and now their Deputy Launching Authority. Here at the harbour we are keen to support the RNLI, lots of those who work for us volunteer on the Padstow boat and we can let them go in the middle of the day.

****

We'd all like to thank Rob (and Sam the Labrador) for his unflappable support and enthusiasm for this book.

LEON BURT
PADSTOW HARBOUR PATROL OFFICER

"…I've been on this River all my life, as a young boy I had my own little punt and gained a lot of local knowledge…"

I've been doing this job for a couple of years, before that I worked at Rock Marine Services. The harbour patrol boat is a RIB with two 200HP Suzuki engines. It's a very capable boat, good in rough weather, good for towing people in, or occasionally fishermen who have got gear caught up.

It's my job to help anyone in distress, stand up paddle-boarders, kite and windsurfers who drift out to sea or visiting yachts not familiar with access to the channel. A lesser part of my job is enforcing the speed limits within the harbour area, various parts have different limits.

For a few years I've been Helm of Rock Lifeboat; my voluntary life and my work experience mesh well together and we get to work with different agencies. I've got a house in Trebetherick. My other 'thing' is mountain biking, I go all over the country and in winter enter some competitions; there's not enough time for that in the summer.

MAD MIKE

IAN 'CHEESER' KITTO, OWNER,
PADSTOW SEA LIFE SAFARIS & WILDLIFE WATCHING COMPANY

"…it's a better job than fishing, I loved trawling but didn't like going away for a week at a time…"

We have five skippers taking tourists to see puffins and dolphins close to the coast and miles out. Our season is from Easter to October half-term. It's nice to keep a boat in the water for those winter days when the weather is suitable. It's a good enough living for a job on the water. Dad was a fisherman potting and netting, I loved inshore potting with him; it was brilliant I might do that again one day.

When I'm off the boat I want to get home, then my pager goes off and I have to go again. I'm proud to be an RNLI crew member on the Padstow boat. I like the buzz and excitement, anyone who tells you they don't like that is a liar. I'm never frightened; I've seen rough sea as a fisherman and I like to help.

My seven year old daughter won't go fishing, she already tells me 'when I'm in charge of the company'…she comes with me as much as she can.

****

A special thanks to Ian for taking Chris out to sea on his boat, enabling him to snap images from the water. DR

LUKE CHOWN

"…when I'm home I like to spend time with my family, and in winter clay pigeon and rough shooting…"

I'm a crewman on the Amanda of Ladram we fish for hake, monk fish and turbot using trammel nets. We land in Newlyn or Brixham. I'm hoping we might start to sail out of Padstow. I am a Padstow man and it's nice to work out of your home port but that's a decision for the skipper. We go twelve months a year and usually away for seven to ten days at a time, sometimes longer.

I'm training to be a navigator with the RNLI - I've been a crewman on the Padstow boat for about fifteen years now, since I was twenty something. The skills are similar to those I use as a fisherman, not too difficult. Plotting courses to casualties is slightly different but it uses similar technology. I can only do RNLI stuff when I'm home so it might take a while.

I'm a sixth generation fisherman, my Uncle Wally was a Commissioner here and I've traced it all back.

PADSTOW HARBOUR COMMISSIONERS
Mike England (6th from L) Chair of Harbour Commissioners, Rob Atkinson (3rd from R) Harbour Master

A number of these faces are seen elsewhere in the Padstow section, as a group they serve an important community role, representing different geographical areas and business interests around the harbour and port. There was a time when twenty-seven Harbour Commissioners participated in legendary meetings that went on till the early hours. Now, following reform, there are ten of us, elected using the Parish electoral role, three from Wadebridge, three from Padstow, three from Rock and the Lord of the Manor, Peter Prideaux-Brune, his seat is usually given to the Harbour Master. There are elections if necessary and Commissioners serve a three year term.

The role is meant to be strategic: deciding on big projects affecting the 'infrastructure' and development of the port. The pontoons on the South Dock, the transformation of the toilet block into the Tourist Information Centre/RNLI shop and the development of the car park at Rock are good examples.
We are meant to look at budgets, set policy direction and delegate responsibility accordingly.

We have our own heavy duty equipment, the Mannin a dredger that clears about ten thousand tonnes of mud a year, and the necessary craft to patrol the port and estuary.

****

The Fishermen's Mission would like to thank Padstow Harbour Commissioners for their sponsorship, which has helped to cover the printing costs of this book.

RYAN PAUL MASTERS
PAUL MASTERS

"…it's nice to see the plaque on the Red Brick Building commemorating Dad…"

Grandad lived in the house my mum and Stepdad live in now. Dad had lived there as well. I wanted to go fishing but after losing my Dad, Grandad wouldn't let me. In the end he let me try it and I've stayed doing it since.

I fish out of Newlyn on the Harvest Reaper, it's more practical for me to live up here with all my family: my girlfriend Samantha and two little ones, Lily and Oliver. I go away for ten days then home for a week. I probably see my children more than some with a nine to five job. It's lonely for both of us: Samantha works for Rick Stein and in a hairdresser. It's tiring. I miss them all.

I had an accident two years ago, it was so rough they couldn't air lift me. My jaw was a bit of a mess, five plates in, two months off work. Then last February I was just about to go to sea, I went over on my ankle and did all the ligaments in, off work for a month with no money. We'd struggled that year. I got hold of the Mission and Keith and Eddie helped me with the month's mortgage. They were brilliant.

COLIN MAIN

"…at seven I just upped and went, skived school everyday to go fishing…"

I didn't come from fishing, Dad was a builder. I went fishing for others, out in a hurricane in 1986 it took nine and a half hours to get back from Lundy. I did eighteen years in the Merchant Navy, worked supply boats to the Falklands at the time of the conflict and then to Scotland on a dredger.

I had a bad accident: I got caught up in an anchor winch. I felt noises, as though my back was breaking. It was my pelvis and leg: now one leg is three-quarters of an inch shorter than the other and my pelvis never mended. They said I'd never walk again, it was three years before I could work again but never went back to sea. I defied them though and worked in steel erecting. I guess I'm lucky to be here.

I've seen the Mission in different ports all around the UK, Newlyn, Ipswich and Scotland. I've just raised £1,800 growing my hair and shaving it all off. My daughter who's a dog groomer cut it off and Steve Kirk shaved my head. Mum is 84, I have seven step-children, thirty-two grand-children, fifty great-grandchildren and fourteen great-great-grandchildren.

JULIAN WILLIAMS
OWNER - DGW SAND CO LTD & the SAND SNIPE

"…I'm not from Padstow, but Hayle, been here thirty years though…"

Dad died a couple of years ago and I decided to take the firm on. We started in Hayle but dredging in Hayle was stopped thirteen years ago. Now we dredge the Padstow channel and the Camel Estuary. 95% of the sand goes for agricultural uses, it's high in calcium and good for the soil. It is also used for cattle bedding and in sand-schools for horses but not for cement.

We dredge into the Sand Snipe, then it's taken to our holding yard at St Merryn. Then sold to farmers direct or to local wholesale suppliers like Jack Kingdon or Graham Carlyon. We supply all across Cornwall, Devon and parts of Somerset.

We work with the Harbour Commissioners: they direct us where to work following surveys and maps of the sea bed. Banks of sand build up in different places due to tides, weather conditions and lots of different factors, it's a continuous task. We have a dredger and re-handler here and a loading shovel in the yard.

JOHN JERMYN
(Left)

"…I'm retiring from fishing now, going to stay on dry land, with three hundred chickens in my field…"

The boat is called the Helen Jane II and I've been her skipper for twelve years now. We use trammel nets for turbot, monk, and brill. We land the fish back into Padstow and it goes by road to a merchant in Appledore, North Devon; some of it ends up at Billingsgate and some goes to the Midlands.

I was born and bred in Padstow and have seen a lot of changes here. I can just remember there being an old fish market here, and the railway. This was the end of the line for the railway and there was a turntable down the other end of the car park for turning the train around. When the railway closed the sheds became fishermen's stores.

He's a thorn in my side! I am glad Wes is taking on the skippering though, the arthritis in my knees means I've got to retire.

WES JERMYN
(Centre)

"…later this year I'm going away for a while and hope to come back and have my own boat…"

I'm taking over skippering the Helen Jane II from Dad for a while. In September I'm going travelling. To the Bahamas to train how to look after yachts people have shares in. It'll still be on the sea, based anywhere, perhaps in Antigua or Greece, I might need that experience if the fishing goes down.

If the bad months outweigh the good months then it's very hard. A while ago there was almost seven months when hardly any north coast boats were able to get out. It's stayed in my memory that the Mission helped me with rent. It's very practical because if there aren't enough good months we can't afford anything. There is no other help for fishermen in that case.

I've always supported Tim and Lisa when they were at the London Inn, got my hoodie there, they even brewed a special ale with St Austell Brewery - which of course I drank - I'll always put towards it if I can. I'm really happy to support other people's efforts.

THE TEAM AT THE LONDON INN

THE TEAM AT THE HARBOUR INN

JOHN PORTER AND LORRAINE CROW.
SNAPPY CRAB

"…everything we sell here is very popular but I don't eat any of it…"

Lorraine sells shellfish. It comes from Jim up the road who is a local wholesaler, we have all sorts, cockles, jellied eels and anchovies, my Grandson who is three loves it all.

I was seven when Dad came here to work for the RNLI full time, previously he'd been coxswain at Spurn Point. John is a ferry driver for the Harbour Commissioners and has a little fishing boat for chasing dreams, he'd previously been a trawlerman in Brixham.

The family are all local, two sisters live a few doors up the road, the other in Wadebridge. My nieces Michaela and Rosie are both on the Lifeboat crew. It's a lovely community here, always looking out for each other. Up country they say they don't know who their neighbour is, well I could tell you everyone who lives in my street. I love the winter months best as there's more time for family.

EDWARD BOLITHO
LORD LIEUTENANT OF CORNWALL,

My family have been in Cornwall for generations, in the nineteenth century in West Cornwall we had business interests in tin mining, tanning, pilchard exporting and banking. We built the North Pier in Newlyn and with that the fishing took off there. In addition there are family links with The Fishermen's Mission, Aunt Norah left money for an 'institute' to be built for the fishermen which until recently housed the Mission in Newlyn and my mother (Elizabeth Bolitho) still volunteers there.

As Lord Lieutenant I am responsible for organising the royal visits: every year the Duke of Cornwall likes to start his visit at a fishing port, in 2015 we were in Padstow. He is particularly interested in agriculture and fishing both traditional industries and communities currently under a fair amount of social and economic pressure. He likes to talk to fishermen and RNLI men directly, keen to understand how people are responding to those pressures and encourage solutions that are sustainable and practical for the future. He cannot get involved politically but is conscious of the human costs of living and working in such tough environments.

JACKIE STANLEY
PROPRIETOR - JACKIE STANLEY ESTATE AGENTS AND HARBOUR HOLIDAYS
(Centre, top)

"…I'm privileged to live here, and be accepted as part of it. My girls have been drawn back to live and work here because of the community spirit…"

I'm very happy to be a sponsor of this book, because it supports local fishermen. We have to look after the local community, and the local work force. If it wasn't for the fishermen supplying goods there wouldn't be livings to be made. They risk their lives, we cannot do without them as our lovely restaurants know.
I trained in corporate estate agency, and set up on my own agency very quietly in 1972. Selling houses first, the lettings business followed. My daughter joined me, she is young and has all the ideas. We are a small family team, believing in old fashioned personal service and someone is on call 24/7. Our reputation is everything to us and people seem to like a small, private business with local knowledge and experience.

I've seen a lot of change. Overlooking the harbour gives plenty of people watching opportunities: people have a different mentality on holiday and it can be hilarious to observe.

****

The Fishermen's Mission would like to thank Jackie for her sponsorship, which has helped to cover the printing costs of this book.

THE NATIONAL LOBSTER HATCHERY
A MARINE CONSERVATION, EDUCATION AND RESEARCH CHARITY

The National Lobster Hatchery on Padstow's quayside, represents something that is important, to fisheries around the world. The Charity's work is about food security, fisheries sustainability and developing forward-thinking approaches to complement existing traditional stock conservation schemes. Our approach is three-pronged: an active stocking programme involving the release of thousands of cultured lobsters into the wild; a broad targeted programme of innovative research and an education outreach programme.

Human populations are at an all-time high, and fish stocks under unprecedented pressure from growing demand for seafood and advancing technology with which to catch it. Lobsters have not been immune to this pressure, in recent decades stocks have been collapsing due to overfishing in some parts of Europe. We are exploring how stock enhancement (the release of robust juveniles, which have been reared through vulnerable early life-stages in the hatchery), increases lobster abundance and how well these interventions add to the productivity of the fishery and help to safeguard its future.

The main outcome of the Charity's work is that fishery stakeholders will be better informed as to how lobster stock enhancement and re-stocking can best contribute to sustainably managed stocks, better-informed conservation policy and more prosperous coastal communities.

IAN MURRAY
FISHERMEN'S MISSION PORT OFFICER S.E. CORNWALL

"…the Mission's work is not always financial, it's a news network for old fishermen too, be it two or two hundred miles away, everybody has news or knows somebody…"

It can make a elderly fisherman's day to have a visit and a chat, passing on information and news. I volunteered for the Mission about six years ago and I've been four years in uniform, my patch covers from Bude, to Looe, to St Mawes, to Padstow and Port Isaac.

I spent thirty-five years fishing but developed knee problems. The Mission helped by putting me in touch with The Dreadnought Unit at Guys Hospital, it's a separate unit of the NHS set up by a Victorian philanthropist to help injured Merchant Navy men and fishermen. The Mission are its agents in the field, helping with forms and cash to get to London. I got my knee fixed quickly, this fast track to help meant I avoided a long wait and could get back to earning my living. If a fisherman doesn't go out to fish, he doesn't get any money coming in.

My wife Jill is a congregational minister and we find that the two roles intertwine well, we help each other.

BAREFOOT MEDIA

"…we are passionate about Cornwall: its community, industry, heritage and landscape…"

Nowadays, Barefoot employs six members of staff, working on PR and digital marketing for a wide array of clients, most of whom are strongly tied to Cornwall's land and sea, beautiful hotels with sea views, restaurants whose chefs choose to serve fantastic Cornish fish on their menus, working farms which have diversified into offering accommodation, weddings and feast nights. In addition there are high profile events such as Padstow Christmas Festival, Polo on the Beach and London Oyster Week.

Through their work at Padstow Christmas Festival, Barefoot is in close contact with the Padstow community - business owners, fishermen, residents and holidaymakers. The Festival is only four days long but, behind the scenes, the Barefoot team works on the Festival most of the year, putting together the brochure and website, and working with the press and media to promote Padstow in what was, historically, one of the town's quietest weekends of the year, but is now its busiest.

MIKE MASTERS AND SARAH ALLEN
ST KEW INN

"…that's what I love about the Mission, they are there for the family afterwards…"

Sarah grew up in Padstow, my parents ran pubs. I was great friends with Dave Masters and his fiancé, he was lost at sea in 1992. His brother Paul was a big personality in Padstow. When he was lost he left behind his wife Linda and two very young children. It was great to see how the Mission stepped in and helped them when she suddenly became a single mum. I worked at Stein's alongside Christine Hope whose son Peter was also lost in 1992; you don't get over that, but to see Padstow pull together for the families is something special.

I've been here ten years, been doing the Envelope Scheme for nine. We put Mission Envelopes on the tables so people can choose to leave some change if they like, no pressure. In small donations like this we've raised about £10,000. All our fish in the restaurant comes from Newlyn, Padstow or Port Isaac. Sometimes you look at the weather out there and think it's awful: there's someone out to sea in these conditions bringing in my fish.

SHARP'S BREWERY

"…we are absolutely rooted in where we live and want to look after it. Rock is the centre of our business and we are here to stay…"

Rachel Williams is Communications Manager. Since I came ten years ago we have more than doubled the size of the workforce. We now provide year round employment and attract a diverse work force from all over the world, but the largest proportion is still from North Cornwall.

It is important to be part of the local community, within say, a ten mile radius of here including both Padstow and Port Isaac. People are attracted to this area by the food and drink. We like to support and promote the hard work that goes into putting that produce on the plate or in the glass.

We've been involved with the Mission for about six years. We saw a really proactive charity, working with a lot of the same people we worked with. When the storms hit a few years ago it impacted on the pubs and the communities and it was shocking to see the coastline, communities and individuals so battered. We are very proud of our association with a charity that aims to look after those people in times of great need.

****

The Fishermen's Mission would like to thank Sharp's Brewery for their sponsorship, which has helped to cover the printing costs of this book.

JEFF HEWITT
OWNER,
CHAPMAN & HEWITT BOATYARD SERVICES AND CRANE HIRE, WADEBRIDGE

"…every morning I come down the road at six o'clock and think, I must do something on my boat to get it in the water…"

I started my working life building small racing dinghies for Westerly Boats and setup this business with my ex, now-deceased partner in 1971. We built this business maintaining and building small local inshore fishing boats but haven't built a new boat here for a number of years. We service and repair boats providing all the associated services, engines for leisure craft and small fishing boats twelve to fourteen metres maximum. We run a small crane hire business from here too.

My customers are from the North Coast: Newquay, Port Isaac, Boscastle and Bude. I know the older generation of Newquay fishermen well. When Gary Eglinton wants to know anything he'll be on the phone Christmas Day, Sunday, 6 am or 10pm, anytime.
In fishing that's how it is, just a way of life, good things and bad things about it.
I hope to reach being seventy-one next week.

Born half a mile away, I've lived in Wadebridge almost all my life. A week in the old railway carriages at Polzeath with Mother, her sister and children was a real outing. My two daughters live locally and I love taking my grandchildren on the Camel Trail.

I've not had my sailing boat in the water for three years.

ROCK FISH
MARTYN HARRIS AND JAN KANE

*"…we do have a very loyal base of regular customers who live locally, some come from Wadebridge
or Port Isaac because the parking here is easy…"*

Jan has worked selling fish here since 1999. I now own Rock Fish with my business partner Martyn.
Previously I'd worked for Dennis Knight since the shop first opened, Dennis was still on the road
then. I've seen generations of the same family, unborn children now at university and some with their
own children. I see a lot die too.

People have become more adventurous: in the last three years we've sold more hake than cod.
People are much better educated about what fish is readily available and keen to see what it tastes
like. I used to be a chef so I talk to customers about how to prepare and cook the fish; it definitely
helps. Our homemade things are popular too: fish pies, fish cakes, hot smoked salmon, sea trout and
mackerel. I make gravadlax and smoked fish pâtés too, people like it very much.

We've got some wonderful restaurants here attracting people with an interest in food to visit the area
and the fishmonger is attractive to them too.

JON BERNASCONI AND KAY GRIFFITHS
OWNERS - OFF THE HOOK FISHMONGERS, WADEBRIDGE

"…being a local Cornish boy, surrounded by water and fishing bringing in this fantastic fish all going up-country. I wanted to keep some of it for our own community…"

Jon trained as a fishmonger with Morrisons: originally I started as a butcher, I really didn't like fish but working on the fish counter was part of the job. I got some training and discovered a passion. Given lots of opportunities to progress. I wanted to stay with fish so I left there with everything I learned and after eighteen months, looking around, we opened here ten months ago.

Mum was born in Port Isaac and went to school with Dennis Knight! We'd wanted to work with someone local but we get our fish from Wing of St Mawes, from Newlyn and occasionally crab and lobster from Browns in Port Isaac.

Kay has caught her passion for fish from Jon: I never knew much about it but now I love to help people learn how to cook it well, try new things and make recommendations. We have a lot of returning customers, from all around this area. Customers are keener now to know where the fish comes from and how it is caught; we use the Cornwall Good Seafood Guide on the wall to help.

Albert is by the till: we haven't got a business without the fishermen, we couldn't do what they do, we're not too good at sea, so want to support the Fishermen's Mission.

TIM MARSHALL
OWNER - ROCK SHELLFISH

*"…a young Marine Biology student came to see Father, he'd seen a way of growing oysters in France.
He tried here but failed and left. In the abandoned mess you could see oysters growing like wildfire…"*

The family have farmed here for five generations. Two of us brothers with families, we'd struggle with
only ninety cows. I'd always enjoyed mucking about with anything fishing: angling, crabbing, boats.
We'd gave the oysters a try initially for a bit of beer money, it worked so we grew it from that.

Seed is bought from a specialist hatchery, then they feed and grow on algae in the river. In bags, sat on
trestles at the bottom of a spring tide, they are always in the water and we can get to them with a tractor
and barge. Years later, they are harvested, washed, sat in UV light for about forty-two hours to get rid of
any coliforms and graded to an EU scale similar to lamb or spuds.

The French will always pay a premium: very little goes abroad, except to Nathan's in Dubai. A little
brand of their own, amazing local demand from chefs and shops, a lot go to London and Birmingham.
There's a limit to expansion though, we can't control the water it's the great imponderable.

THE MARINERS TEAM
NATHAN OUTLAW RESTAURANTS

"…we had a great relationship with Sharps and running a pub together was the next step: exploring the role beer can play as a partner with food, just as wine does…"

Ian Dodgson is General Manager for Nathan Outlaw Restaurants. In 2013 Sharps approached us asking if we'd be interested in developing a joint venture at The Mariners. As a result we have grown a symbiotic relationship. Like us, they deliver great flavours through beer, as we do through Nathan's food. The main thing is people enjoying their night: eating, drinking and being looked after by good people.

We've tried to pull together the ethos of both businesses. It is also about the staff. We want people to enjoy their working life. The whole package matters to us: not just pay but training, working hours, good time off, making sure staff are eating properly - we've got a nutritionist coming to help us structure good staff meals.

This industry need not be a labour of love, with stupid hours and no sleep. We need to attract and retain good people, developing career paths and opportunities. Front of house needs to become a respected career choice, not just a fill in or holiday job - we hope we are pushing industry standards upwards.

ROCK RNLI

"…currently the largest crew we've ever had, twenty-two operational crew members and next year we celebrate twenty-five years since our station opened…"

Stuart Robertson is on the shore crew at Rock RNLI and their Press Officer. I grew up here, my earliest memories are of sailing on the Camel Estuary. My father owned Westerly Boats, which built Cornish Crabbers and Shrimpers from wood and fibreglass.

The RNLI discovered a need for a lifeboat station at Rock. The All Weather Boat at Padstow was being called to shouts they couldn't reach so a D-Class boat was needed in addition. It's rare for the RNLI to set up new stations. They put in an experimental station on site with a temporary boat for a year, while the crew was formed and trained. Once it was found to be worthwhile we had our own boat.
This is the third one. Our existing boathouse was built following an appeal for voluntary funds.

People really want to volunteer for and be part of the RNLI. Everyone on the crew has to be working or living within the boundaries of our parish. The more crew we have the better chance of getting to an incident. We often work in tandem with the big boat at Padstow

JAMES NATHAN
HEAD CHEF ST ENODOC HOTEL, 2008 AMATEUR MASTERCHEF WINNER

"…I adore cooking, like an artist, with a blank chopping board, a knife and an onion; sauté this, add that, cooking by intuition…"

I'm a self taught chef, my mother was a very passionate cook, a real Delia in the '70s. She was into organic early, grew her own vegetables. We were a big family, six of us children and she would cook for thirty on Christmas Day, an inspirational woman. Cooking is, as Rick Stein told me once, an affliction, a hard and demanding one.

I like good simple food cooked well. I like to go out on my mountain bike into the woodlands in spring. The dearth of winter is gone, the wild garlic with its noisy clamouring scent heralds the spring. I love to forage for things to cook, it forces you to cook with the seasons, to appreciate what's around you. This is a lost art.

I moved to Cornwall for the seafood and fish and I am hoping to stay here and settle, I have a little daughter now too.

PADSTOW CHRISTMAS FESTIVAL EVENT TEAM

"…it started eleven years ago with a group of us throwing ideas around about how we could bring extra business to Padstow in the slower season…"

Tina Evans leads the Event Team. The Padstow Christmas Festival started at a time when other places were doing food and drink festivals. We decided ours would be on the first Thursday in December aiming to kick start Christmas. It's now a firm favourite in the diaries, people book accommodation for the whole week and make a holiday of it.

The Festival has evolved but one strong element present from the start is to qualify, all stallholders must be based in Cornwall or Devon. We want to showcase the excellence in Cornwall and Devon. We also need to keep the Festival fresh and appealing to our large number of repeat visitors. This year we used our database for market research and have tweaked the way we select stallholders, meaning there will be a lot of new ones coming in which is very exciting. A recent article assessed the Festival as bringing £5 million to the local economy, so we have succeeded in the original aim to develop business in Padstow in the quiet season.

We are very lucky to have Andrew Stephens of the Old Ship involved. It's lovely to have some youth on our side, otherwise all areas are run by this wonderful group of volunteers who are each responsible for a specific area of the Festival. It is amazing to think the Chef's Demonstration Area is run by a volunteer, while others manage the merchandising.

****

The Fishermen's Mission would like to thank the Festival Team for their gift of a table to promote and sell this book at the 2018 Festival.

FRIENDS OF PADSTOW CHRISTMAS FESTIVAL

"…we want make sure the whole community benefits…"

Tina explains another aspect of the Festival Team. As a group we also run four charity events during the year. The aim is to raise money for local community groups so the success of the Festival gets into the wider Padstow community, beyond the business and hospitality community.

Traditionally we have raised huge amounts of money with Ladies Days at Treglos, Charity Golf Days, a Ladies Lunch at Paul Ainsworth's and this year there are one or two new events. Each day during the Festival we have a huge basket of goods for a massive raffle which raises hundreds for the Friends. We then organise a Donation Evening when the money from these events is donated to local schools, Brownies, Cubs, Sea Cadets and the Christmas Lights every year which cost thousands to put on.

THIS TABLET IS ERECTED IN MEMORY OF THE FIVE
YOUNG MEN OF PADSTOW WHO DIED IN TWO FISHING
BOAT DISASTERS OF 22ND NOV. AND 29TH NOV. 1992.

NEIL HARDING
ARNOLD MURT
DAVID MASTERS
PETER HOPE
PAUL MASTERS

PADSTOW FISHERMENS APPEAL FUND.

IN MEMORY
LOST AT SEA
CLIFFORD COUTSOUBOS
✝ 24.11.89
"GREY FLAMINGO"
JOHN HARRIS
✝ 3.3.91
"LADY SYLVIA"

THE HOPE FAMILY
(L–R) James, Adrian, Christine, Tracey
Peter

Christine is Pete's Mum. It's horrendous, twenty six years since he went down, he was twenty-three.
We don't know exactly what happened. It took two weeks to find him, we weren't allowed to see
him and then there were weeks before we could bury him. Most of the time you can dismiss the
horror. Even now I just well up sometimes. I did a Master Baker's course at Camborne College when
I was forty. I have my own catering business now.

Pete was quiet, 6' 2", size fourteen feet, he came back from Hull once with one shoe: we still have
that. He'd joined the Lifeboat, Trevor England was Coxswain then, he said "we go out to save
people's lives and it's heartbreaking when we can't save one of our own." I remember that.

Adrian is Peter Henry's Father. He was aiming for a good life, fishing. I see his picture every day,
'Mornin' Pete, Good Night Pete' I say, he's still with us, such is life. The sea is a terrible place;
I know that from working in the Merchant Navy and fishing.

Tracey was twenty-five. I had to tell my Mum he's not coming back. Dad was out looking for him,
we'd been in the harbour office all night, we heard it over the radio. I was drunk on and off for three
months. I had good friends and family help me through. If I sit and think I choke up, they found him
the day after my birthday. I've been a chef and recently retrained at night school and Truro College
to do accounts.

James was fifteen. I'm in the Merchant Navy now, I've been fishing with Sid Porter. It hit me hard a
few years afterwards. I think of Pete every day, it almost stopped me from going to sea. I didn't want
to worry my parents. Mother didn't want me to go but she's glad I did.
It's been a good career and it has helped them a bit.

KIRSTY MASTERS AND DEBORAH RICHARDS
(L–R) Kirsty, Deborah

"…this project introduced us to each other, it was lovely to meet a younger woman who cherished family and community like I do, yet we are so different…"

Kirsty turned the recorder on. Parts of this project have been challenging: I heard harrowing stories from some, great optimism from others, an all encompassing range really. Listening back to the tapes I sensed the challenge to write sensitively, to be considerate of people who had generously trusted me with difficult, almost private feelings. I wanted them to feel I'd honoured their trust.

My perceptions of fishing haven't changed: my knowledge and understanding has. At last, I had a chance to shout about our traditional industries. How they demand hard physical work in conditions most would not tolerate today. It's important, every effort is made to sustain our small remote coastal communities for the future. Fishing is very like farming, boats or land owned and worked across families, passed down from one generation to another. It's a big thing when someone decides to get out. People die in farming but somehow death at sea seems even worse.

The writer who encouraged and mentored me to write died young of leukaemia. I swam this estuary from Padstow to Rock for Macmillan for her. With her in my head and you by my side I hope I've done Padstow proud.

****

"…the day we weren't down on the docks anymore I missed it: we just had the biggest laugh down there with them all…"

Deborah turned the recorder on. I just loved being part of the Fishermen's Mission team on this project. The Mission means so much to my family, from when my Uncle died. I just wanted to help. I'd shown people the Newlyn book, some people were really up for it, others less forthcoming.

I'd never done anything like this before. I've learned that Facebook is amazing for organising people. We don't have any fishermen in my immediate family now. I'd always known people go to sea, but trying to organise something practical like this around their fishing trips emphasised how difficult this life is for the families.

Recently I'd started thinking our community spirit was dying out. As a result of the book project I think it's probably stronger than I thought. When there's a tragedy the united front is very obvious and visible: a supportive bond. It is less visible in everyday life but it is still here, I've seen it again. Spending more time with the fishermen I realised how strong and hopeful it was. I'm quite old fashioned in the way I think and loyalty, family and community are really important to me and should be kept going. I'm looking forward to the launch day that'll be a great community time.

RICK AND KATIE TOOGOOD

"…this is a working fishing town, our staff, our friends everyone is connected, the community has accepted us and it's nice to give back…"

This is our home now, if at all possible we want to be a part of this community. It's nice to walk down the street and people to say hello, that doesn't happen in London. We live in the town, drink locally, a lot of our staff live here and they've helped us to integrate, it's quite scary when you first move down. Our discount Cockle Cards are for locals and recently we started sponsoring Padstow U12 Girls Football team. Customers at Prawn on the Lawn support the Lobster Hatchery through a donation scheme.

I've spent a day out on the boat with Johnny Murt, it is bloody hard physical work, it's very isolated too. Through social media we can shout about the fish and the men who bring it in. Helping in a small way to reduce isolation by communicating more, developing a wider understanding of the jump from sea to plate.

Sponsoring the book is a different way for us to support this community. It's our gift, helping to show how valuable this community is to us, now and for the future.

****

The Fishermen's Mission would like to thank Rick and Katie for their sponsorship, which has helped to cover the printing costs of this book.

PAUL AINSWORTH
OWNER No6, THE PADSTOW TOWNHOUSE AND ROJANO'S IN THE SQUARE

"…we only use fish from Cornish waters, somehow it doesn't seem right to bring fish in from Scotland when we've got such variety here…"

Paul, first left. My Grandad was a trawlerman and lifeboatman from the North-West near Poulton-le-Fylde. Dad was born into fishing but didn't want to fish, that's quite a big decision in a family. As a result the RNLI and the Fishermen's Mission are special charities to me. There's no more powerful force than the sea, sometimes boats can be tossed around like bits of paper.

I went out with Brian Bate, just in the estuary here, it was by no means rough sea but it is dangerous, hard graft and each time they risk their lives to bring home this wonderful produce.
It's hard on the families too.

I was introduced to the Mission in Newlyn in 2011 when I visited as part of The Great British Menu. Just seeing all the names of men lost at sea in that building there, recognising some Padstow names was incredibly moving. We did those winning dishes for four nights here and raised money for the Mission. They work sensitively to support fishing families in a straightforward way.

Port Isaac

GEORGE 'CLEAVEY' CLEAVE

"…I like making people aware of quality fish and its preparation, I like cooking but I'm not a chef…"

I've worked with fish since I was thirteen, it's good to learn a trade in Cornwall instead of working away. I went to Australia with a friend: within a week I'd found work as a fish monger in Melbourne. They put me on really good money, it taught me a massive amount I wouldn't have learned if I'd stayed in Cornwall.

Missing Cornwall I came home: wanting to teach people about the fishing industry and fish preparation. Today people are more aware of quality fish due to Instagram and TV chefs, wanting to learn how to handle it. We need to explain the real costs of putting quality fish on plates.

A unit came up in the Fish Cellars, at the bottom of the village in Port Isaac. For a year I've been refurbishing it, aiming to open a 'school' to teach fish preparation.

I love fishing myself and have a lot of friends in the fishing community. I speak to them out at sea using Facebook and Snapchat. That immediate connection between fisherman and merchant means I pass on news of what the catch is.

DAVE PHILLIPS

"…I'm not very good on the sea, I'm a little bit the one hanging over the side…"

I'm the van driver for Dennis Knight's Fish Merchant. My mother was a Cornish lady and my dad was from Wales. I've lived in St Minver, the village just over there all my life.

I love the fish, I started eating fresh fish when I started working here, it's such an eye opener, absolutely gorgeous. My wife does a hake dish which she bakes in the oven with a breadcrumb top and garlic.

I love my work and my life, it's so lovely being in Cornwall and to have the fresh fish.
I love meeting the people. I don't really do exciting, maybe delivering fish to one of the posh houses for the odd wedding. I had a tree fall down on me at Altarnun once, that was quite exciting.

JAQUI STEWART
(below)

"…Albert sits on the counter with the forks and spoons…"

Just Shellfish is in the Cellars at Port Isaac. I pick crab for Jeremy and Liz Brown and their children Tom and Lisa. I came from Swanwick in Derbyshire when my son, who'd been here for ten years, announced I was going to be a grandparent. As it was my only family I moved here.

When anyone says 'keep the change' it always goes in the Albert for the Fishermen's Mission, everyone puts in small change, but today he got given a £5 note.

ROSIE BROGAN
(above)

" …I walk out every day and look at that harbour, it never changes and I want that for my children…"

I've lived here all my life, I come from a fishing family going back generations. I've chosen to be by the sea, unable to imagine my children not being part of this. Lots have gone away for work, but I work here and bring up my children Daisy two, and Lily six, in Port Isaac, by the sea. There's a growing primary school here, years ago it nearly closed but now there are a lot more kids, it's still not a large school.

People don't often come back here once they've moved away but there are a lot of others coming in, mostly people who want to live by the sea too, so the community is growing.

When the girls are older we might have to move to give them other options. This is a safe, happy community that keeps an eye out for everyone's children, that's a rural and remote thing. The Community Lunch started up recently in the Village Hall and I just wanted to be part of that and join in to do something for everyone.

JOHN COLLINS

"…yes, I enjoy coming to work every day really…"

I was born in Port Isaac and lived here all my life. I started working Saturdays and school holidays for Dennis Knight Fishmongers, when I was thirteen. Ten or twelve years ago I bought the business from Dennis when he retired. George Cleave works here as the manager, he started working for me when he was thirteen and with the exception of a year off in Australia has worked here ever since.

Seeing good quality fish come in, mainly from Cornwall is very enjoyable. I meet lots of different people in wholesale and retail. I like all the different fish, we sell favourites like John Dory, turbot or gurnard and the tuna which we get imported!

Currently we have fifty or sixty restaurants on our books most of them in Cornwall but a few over the border into Devon and one or two in London. The fish counter in the Cellars is open most days selling a wide range of fish to anyone who wants to buy.

I've been a member of the RNLI Port Isaac crew for many years, the last nine as Deputy Launching Authority, Nikki B, my wife is the longest serving lady member of the Life Boat crew.

PORT ISAAC COMMUNITY LUNCH TEAM

"…there was a need in the village for something like this, people were being taken elsewhere…"

Caroline Cleave (1st L). After a bit of discussion it was decided there were enough of us to commit to doing a Community Lunch once every couple of months or so, providing something the village didn't have. The aim was to share food and each other's company.

Things that happen in the village need to be inclusive, we need to share the wisdom and skills of older people with the energy and determination of the younger ones. One of our older ladies is one of the best cooks in the village, with loads of experience cooking for charity but isn't keen on running around the Village Hall serving, so others do that bit.

Some of us have more confidence than others: so it's lovely when someone who doesn't think they could volunteer comes forward and says, "I'd like to be part of the Lunch team". Sharing the buzz of volunteering and enabling people to give something back is important.

We are hoping it will become a regular feature: keen to encourage people to enjoy all aspects while constantly looking at ways of sustaining it.

****

Thank you for the donation to Mission funds from the raffle that day: the lunch was lovely too. DR

BOB BULGIN
CHAIRMAN PORT ISAAC RNLI

"…Port Isaac is a very special place to me, I've been here thirty eight years, my home is here…"

When I hung up my boots after a varied and interesting working life I became more involved with the RNLI. I started as a Press Officer, that was twenty-five years ago now.

What stands out is the dedication of the crew to the actual rescue work that's carried out and the danger to which they go to without thinking, taking on the challenge, that's got to be admired. There are strong links with the fishing community too, as they also risk their lives. I have also written a little history of Port Isaac Lifeboat.

NATHAN OUTLAW

"…my secret weapon are the suppliers I have and the fishermen who bring fish to me…"

I am a seafood chef based in Cornwall for the last twenty years. Eighty per cent of the fish we buy is from Cornwall, predominantly Port Isaac, Newlyn and Looe. We buy crab and lobster direct from Port Isaac fishermen. I don't need to go far to get the best crab and lobster in the world. We buy wet fish from smaller boats, one or two men teams on day boats is the best fish.

Being fresh and knowing the chain from sea to plate is important. I'm very fortunate being based in a county where so many species are available and the fishermen have the necessary expertise.

The community support here is massive. Anyone who has visited a small village like Port Isaac will sense that straight away. It's a close knit community supporting one another, fishermen and their families we all look after each other and that's the way it should be.

I have supported the Fisherman's Mission since way back when I first started cooking seriously for Rick Stein in the late '90s. It made complete sense: a charity that supported the fishing families through hard times. My in-laws are in a fishing related business, for me it's a no brainer.

SHARON OUTLAW

"…Nathan came to visit us in Kent where he was brought up and we still lived, "oh I could do with a PA." I said jokingly, as you do, "well I'll do it!…"

When I was at school, young women were told you were a mother and a wife, if you did a job it was really for pin money. Ambition wasn't born in me until a lot later when I realised there was more out there.

Not having done university after school I went back to do a three year degree and a Post Graduate Teacher Training year. Learning in later life was enjoyable but worried me a bit because the young people seemed so bright, they knew big words but had little experience of life like mine. I benefitted from that experience though, it meant I could deal with harder situations, it made me more resilient.

I didn't know anything about fish and I don't eat it either! Most people find that hilarious! To me fishing was trawlers: I didn't know about small, family owned day boats, where they go out alone and risk everything to do the job. The fishing community history is fascinating, where families have done this for years and years, whole towns and villages built up around this one activity. It's wonderful these traditions are still carried on, unique, hopefully it will never stop and there's nothing else like it.

PORT ISAAC RNLI

"…I love the RNLI: it's an awesome thing to be part of, a passionate crew, land based committee and even more passionate following from our supporters…"

Damien Bolton (3rd L) is Senior Helm with Port Isaac RNLI. This is my twenty-second year on the crew here, my great-grandparents were affiliated to the RNLI and dad is Life Boat Operations Manager.

The crew is quite mixed: eighteen members, four active helms and fourteen crew from a wide variety of backgrounds, two thirds local families and a third newbies. We have a coasteering company owner, a fisherman, a fish merchant, a naval officer, electricians, builders and a shop owner.
All jobs allowing crew to stay in the village within the distance guidelines.

It is a D class boat, requiring two or three crew but we usually go with three or four as this is an exposed and treacherous patch. The boats have improved over time with more technology and we can work with the all weather boat at Padstow if needed.

I've seen memorable shouts, some sad and tragic. Members of our crew have earned awards from the Fishermen's Mission and RNLI Medals for Gallantry.

JEREMY BROWN
Maverick

"…I took it over, and now this has a nice handed down feel about it…"

Five or six generations of my family have fished here, pilchard and herring, now crab and lobster. My son Tom, named after Grandfather, is taking on the fishing from me. Our daughter Lisa taken over the shop, Just Shellfish in the Cellars in Port Isaac. Grandfather ran and managed the pilchard business and smokehouse for Pawlyn's of Mevagissey when they had interests here.

We used to pick eighteen tons of whole crab a year, phenomenal, my wife, my daughter and another lady. We supplied retail and hotels then, now we can't get the people who want to pick. The shop is open from Easter to Christmas and sells what we bring in, we do keep a few prawns, cray fish and mussels, always something to offer if we do run out of crab and lobster. If we've fished more it goes to market via Camel Fish, handy for us, in Rock.

It's hard to imagine being anywhere else, friends, family and work all nearby. We like to travel a bit, last year we drove over two thousand miles across Europe in our coach built camper van: get behind the wheel and go!

TOM BROWN
Maverick

NICOLA 'NIKKI B' BRADBURY

"…Make way young lady, the men are launching the lifeboat" they'd shout, "not without me they're not" I'd reply. "Oh my God, she's going…"

Great Great Granfer George McOwen was on the old Padstow lifeboat for forty-nine years. In 1996 while working behind the bar in The Golden Lion, a crew man came in after a shout, saying "it's no place for a woman, you'd never make it maid" that was *the* challenge, the first woman on this crew and now twenty one years on, among its longest serving members.

We had a shout, Easter Sunday 2012, an adult son had been washed off the cliffs at Tregardock, a really snarly place. The father threw a life ring to the son but both got washed into the sea. The father, Peter, drowned and died. The son, Paul, having kept his father's body out of the snarly water for almost an hour was exhausted. Eventually we got Paul airlifted by helicopter, very very reluctant to leave his father behind. We were able to bring Peter home to his grateful family.
That's what I got my Gallantry Medal for.
You need to be able to box the emotions, which I can do until we start talking about dogs.

It's not for everyone though, a lot of commitment, training, time away from wives, husbands and children: to be recommended though, one hundred percent.

TREVOR BEARE

"…I've enjoyed my time at sea and still looking forward to going back…"

I started fishing out of Rock in the early 1970's. After ten years I joined the Merchant Navy spending time on coasters venturing as far away as West Africa and Brazil. For a few years now I've been fishing part time out of Port Gaverne. Unfortunately I bought a boat without a licence and since discovered it's cheaper to buy another boat with a licence, rather than bring the other up to modern requirements.

I am the longest serving crew member of Port Isaac RNLI, joining first in 1972. I was already fishing then and wanted to give something back. Knowing a lot of people in Newquay RNLI and being too far for their shouts they pointed me here. I'm on the shore crew nowadays: assisting with launching, keeping the station up to scratch, whatever is needed.

This morning I was talking to some of our local RNLI Beach Lifeguards who have been to the Gambia where I spent quite a lot of time. I know the lifeboat station there and in summer their beaches are full of people too.

JOEY AND RICHARD THOMAS
Sharic Mar

DENNIS KNIGHT

"…I started a fish business here, on October 11th 1970 with a Morris 1000 van, ACV 268V…"

For twenty nine years I plied my wares on the road, all round Launceston and Bodmin.
Later I opened a shop in Port Isaac, another in Rock and a wholesale business.

I got a great buzz from being out and about. I saw terrific hidden talent; people building clocks, model boats, beautiful tapestries and embroideries. I made many lovely friends, when I gave up I had to find an excuse to go back to Bodmin or Launceston to see them.

I've seen lots of changes, traffic, more roundabouts and roads. When I started, the housewife would come out with her plate: I'd sell her three whole plaice, she'd skin and fillet them. When I finished home delivering the housewife expected me to skin, fillet and pin bone those plaice. The changes came as women went out to work. Eventually I rarely saw my customers: there'd be a plate outside the backdoor, money in the shed. I put the fish in the cold box, took the money and not see them till the next school holidays.

I was delighted my Saturday boy John (Collins), bought the business, it's still going from strength to strength. He carried on that tradition; George came to work for him when he was 14 or so, traditions, handing on but responding to the modern.

JULIAN BROWN AND PAUL GREGORY

"…we don't push the weather like we used to, do we?…"

It's the place, the number of locals is dropping, nowhere for anyone to be brought up in Port Isaac anymore. Every house goes to an outsider or as a second home. As a child we'd be on the beach all day, stay around the boats and fishermen, then when Dad came in we'd go home.

There's a young one here who hasn't had the enthusiasm knocked out of him yet, his father (Callum Greenhalgh) is a fisherman here. Then there's my nephew Tom. My own son, chose a 'proper job', he's earning more than me crewing on a super yacht, he might come back one day, but he's still on the sea.

It might be too long to wait, we are getting too old; age has changed things. We try to work a bit more cleverly now, just taking it slower, a lot slower. It's a longer winter but we just take our time to do things properly now.

LISA BROWN

"…Some of our customers saw the lady who was here before my Mum, they've seen my Mum and now they are seeing me…"

My job is a crab picker, I've done it for lots of years and recently started taking over from my Mum while she helps with the babysitting on the days the children are not in nursery. Our little shop, Just Shellfish is in the Fish Cellars in Port Isaac, we sell the fresh crab and lobsters caught by my brother Tom. Sometimes in the summer we get crab from my Uncle Julian too.

We break off the legs and claws, crack open the body picking out all the meat with a teaspoon. It's quite labour intensive and can take a while to get the hang of it making sure you don't get sinewy bits or shell in with the meat. We smooth the brown meat, wash the shells and pack it all back in. In the height of the summer we get through four boxes containing about 30kg daily of crab and we sell it all.

Keeping this traditional feel is important to me and it means I live in the village where I grew up and my children might do the same one day, but that's up to them.

MARC & BETH KENDALL
GENERAL MANAGERS THE GOLDEN LION PORT ISAAC

"…In Wales I lived on a mountain, so nowhere near the sea…"

We've been here eighteen months. We like being here in the middle of the village. Cruel Coppinger also lives here, he arrived from Denmark, half smuggler half pirate in 1753 many in Port Isaac report meeting his spirit.

A few months after we arrived, a vat of boiling hot water mysteriously fell off the stove all over Marc, left him swimming in boiling water, eight weeks off work followed. Searches near these steps down to the tunnels revealed no treasure: suddenly a rusty but modern 10p coin appears in front of everyone's eyes: not there when we first looked.

Many Port Isaac people have met the spirit of Cruel Coppinger. RNLI crew colleagues, Damien Bolton, Nickki B and John Collins have all come across him. There's lots still to learn of the history and tales of the tunnels under Port Isaac that come up into the Bloody Bones Bar. We host meetings of various village groups and welcome visitors upstairs.

I joined the Lifeboat recently, it's a ten second run when the pagers go. The sea changes every single day and there's always something to train for.

GEOFF PROVIS

"…I couldn't afford to go fishing. I emigrated to Bodmin and became a police cadet instead. I did thirty years in the Police and retired twenty-two years ago…"

For generations my family were harbour masters and fishermen. They came to Port Isaac in the days of sail, when this was a busy commercial port. They brought coal from Wales, salt for the pilchard trade, limestone for the kilns and exported slate from Delabole. The commerce of the county and country when the seas were motorways.

The 'erring' - Silver Darling - shoals arrived in the autumn, south from Wales and the north, this was their southern limit, caught using drift nets. Pilchards came in summer, up from Biscay this was their northern limit caught by seining, in their millions and trillions. This fishing was as important to Cornwall economically, socially and politically as tin mining.

Since I retired my home village has decayed and changed its character. As a young man I knew the people down here. In winter it's like walking through a grave yard and feels very lonely, even in the summer there's no one familiar. When I saw what was happening to the village I decided to write some books and preserve the history to give back.

PORT ISAAC GOLDEN CIRCLE

MAUREEN WOODS

We came to Port Isaac from Lancashire and bought the Drug Store opposite the old school. We also sold Fish and Chips. There was a takeaway downstairs, a restaurant upstairs and the Drug Store at the side, we employed lots of local people over the years we were there.

JOAN MURRAY

"…I can tell you now, with good heart, dear of him, because he ain't here any more…"

Uncle Joe was a Port Gaverne fisherman, Lifeboat Coxswain between 1910 and 1920 I think. One day waiting and watching for him to come in I noticed how Uncle's boat was low in the water. The boat came in full of sacks of white flour which was scarce during the war, it had been recovered from another boat. "Uncle, that should go to the Coastguards." That week the ladies in Port Isaac made lovely splits and white bread. "Now, you've not seen anything have you Joan, and you're not to tell anyone now."

JILL O'CONNOR

I've been living here for over sixty years, I came from London, seems a long ago time now. We were very friendly with the Rowe family, a big fishing family here. My son John idolised Bruce and Charles Rowe and learned everything he knew about fishing from them. They died too young.

It's sad there are so few youngsters coming into fishing, it's hard long days starting at five or six in the morning and home seven or eight in the evening. Often it's a long winter with no money coming in. Fishermen often have to find other jobs in the winter and work very hard through the summer when they can fish to earn enough.

JANET CHADBAND

I don't come from fishing, I grew up in the village. My father was a dairy farmer and had a milk round so he knew everybody.

One day Father obtained a redundant boat, brought it home, made some sections to divide it, turned it upside down so it became a warm airy pigs house. Nothing going to waste.

ROWENA 'NINA' OLIVER

I was born in 1930, Father was a fisherman and he sold his fish around Perranporth to some of the big hotels there.

LILIAN THOMAS

ANNIE PHILP

"…I didn't marry anyone, I kept running…"

I've lived in Port Isaac from six weeks old until now, always loved being here. I'm on a lot of committees in the village, probably all the Committees, and enjoy it very much. After going to Camborne Tech my work life was for the NHS in Learning Disabilities: I loved my job.

There are lots of the Philp family in Canada, I've been four times, to the Yukon. It's a popular Cornish name, more down West than up here so I'm encouraging my family to get on!

You can go to Canada or wherever you want in the world but coming back is special, you're in a lovely place. I love it when it's full in summer, not everybody's cup of tea but I love it. Children fishing in the harbour, people sharing our world if just for two weeks maybe, that's got to be good, it's not ours but to share with people is lovely.

YVONNE CLEAVE

My father was a fisherman, not a Port Isaac man, a yachtsman and a coastguard man. Mother's side were all Port Isaac fishermen, her father earned the Silver Medal and Bar for saving life at sea before the life boat came to Port Isaac.

I remember the herrings coming and being taken down as a child to see all the silver darlings being shaken out of the nets. I knew then you could have a new coat. They were called silver darlings because they were all silver shining in the evening from the oil lamps high up on the boats.

Before tourism took over all families lived down in the village, we all played on the beach, roamed the valleys and picked primroses and decorated the chapels.

If you swam out too far what the old fishermen would say, "come in maid you are too far out", all the fisherman looked after the little children - Happy Days.

IAN CAMPBELL HONEY

"…I entered The Fish PI competition in the village last year, a famous chef was one of the judges and I won…"

My parents were married in Scotland, where I was born, we came to Port Isaac when my father was Yacht Master for the Duke of Sutherland and the Duke of Westminster, I've lived here almost all my life.

I was apprenticed to a building firm as a carpenter and joiner in Wadebridge, fishing has been my life time hobby. A bit of netting, rod and line for bass, mackerel and plaice. Nothing too spectacular, two or three miles out in an old rowing boat with an outboard engine. I've been as far as an island off Tintagel, about six miles away where the pollock is good.

Last year there was a competition, for the best fish pie in the village. I can't remember what I put in it but I won. Cooking is something I've always enjoyed, roasts, fish, omelettes and scrambled eggs, lots of different things really.

FISHERMAN'S FRIENDS

The Fisherman's Friends of Port Isaac were discovered by a music producer of Universal/Island Records back in 2009, singing sea shanties down by the harbour as they had done on a Friday evening for many years. The Fisherman's Friends specialise in songs from the seven seas, befitting their nautical North Cornish coastal roots.

All members of the band's original line-up lived locally and were old friends from schooldays. From the very start, as our name implies, the group consisted entirely of fishermen and their friends, who were in the main, ex and current lifeboat men or coastguards. None gave up their 'day jobs' in the years following the signing by the record label. The music has involved us in many projects and taken us to exciting places, including a TV documentary, several albums (one of which was the highest selling UK folk CD of all time!) a chart entry, a book about our story, UK wide tours, appearances at the Albert Hall, Festival Hall and on the Pyramid stage at Glastonbury Festival, the 'Best Tradition' award at the BBC Folk Awards, and numerous national festivals, TV and radio appearances.
Early 2019 will see the release of a 'feel good' movie, 'The Fisherman's Friends', based on our story.

HAROLD N STOKES AND EILEEN ROBINSON
VOLUNTEER FUNDRAISERS

"…and no, we're not married…"

Norman is a Yorkshireman from near Middlesborough. My business is based in Camelford, we make the biggest range of brake hoses for motor cars in the world. Eileen comes from London, I was a home carer for eighteen years, we don't have much fish in Wembley. We both live in Kilkhampton.

On the evening when the Fishermen's Friends sing in Port Isaac in aid of the Mission we put on our tabards and take our buckets to collect money. We've built it into a fun competition between us over the past five or six years. She goes ahead and I follow on, everybody gives her the money of course, but I still follow on behind collecting more "we've paid" they say - a few young ladies will give me some. People seem to like it, we've just added humour to the proceedings.

Eileen gets about £900 in her bucket, I probably get £100 or so but for just one evening that's not bad. We liked the camaraderie of the people we meet connected with the Fishermen's Mission and the connection with the people they help, it's a very direct charity.

DUGALD SPROULL

CHAIRMAN PORT ISAAC HARBOUR COMMISSIONERS

"…as a child I was almost brought up in the Cellars, with Julian Brown's grandfather watching over us and making withy pots…"

I was born in Port Isaac and have lived in the same house ever since, my father was the local Doctor. He sent us away to school aged nine, with a lot of pressure to join a profession. After university I joined a firm of solicitors in Bodmin and been there ever since. My brother was a teacher and later went commercial fishing out of Padstow. All I wanted to do was come home.

I'm an original member of Port Isaac Fishermen Ltd, a co-operative set up to keep the Fish Cellars for the benefit of the village when Pawlyn's the big merchants pulled out in the 1960's. The Cellars are now let out to various businesses. In the early days everyone was encouraged to be a member, you could buy all sorts of things there, oilers, ropes and boots etc.

Now none of the younger ones want to keep it going, they aren't interested, it is worrying as gradually everyone is getting older and giving up fishing.

CAROLINE CLEAVE
PORT ISAAC ARTIST

"…I grew up in a very creative household but it wasn't until five years ago after a life defining moment I was able to totally commit to being an artist…"

I'd trained as an art teacher, moved to Cornwall, had my three gorgeous boys and always managed to paint and exhibit, fulfilling that artistic part of me. Within a year of deciding to discontinue teaching and concentrate on art, I was picked up by a British designer called Emma Ball. She works nationally and internationally and has taken my work to a level I could never have hoped for.

The theme of my work is integral to the Fishermen's Mission. I'm really interested in the fact that the crab, lobster and fish being brought in today has never changed. It has sustained our small village community for hundreds of years. Our village is changing, the fleet is shrinking we've got young men wanting to carry on family traditions of fishing but finding it hard. The way the produce is presented has changed, fabulous chef's passionate to demonstrate that trail from sea to plate but the heart of it, the central thing, the lobster, crab or fish hasn't changed. It's that essential, single sustaining produce that I'm focussing on in my work: nothing else, except perhaps a plate or a bit of blue fishing rope.

****

Our days in Port Isaac were made much easier by Caroline's enthusiasm, and hospitality. We started there on a very cold, wet and windy April morning. Thank you Caroline, Jon and George for your welcome in Port Isaac, tea and warmth never felt so good. DR

CALLUM, TRACEY & WILLIAM GREENHALGH

"…Fishing is such a hard life, a financial struggle and bad weather is always beyond your control, still it would be nice to pass it on…"

Tracey's family have been fishermen for generations. We have a small cafe and shop in the village where the majority of the catch goes. After education, London's bright lights called, I just hated it, so came home, met Callum and that was it.

There are a quarter of the boats in Port Isaac now compared to when Callum started. Where it used to be crews of two or three, now it's one person, a solitary existence. It has been a long winter.

Our hope is to develop fishing into a sustainable activity, running a smaller slower boat, we are trying to preserve the lobster fishery for the next generation. Cornish Lobster is well known and held in high regard because it lives longer out of water, therefore making it more viable for transportation.

William is fourteen. I first started with Dad, and slowly saved up for a boat of my own. Determined to become a fisherman. There aren't many my age who fish. I have a friend, we go out together, just the two of us. According to Tracey, being outside, having fun, messing around in boats, drilled in safety is much better than playing on the Xbox: her fondest memories are of her own childhood in Port Isaac doing the same thing.

SEA,
SALT
and
SOLITUDE

This book is dedicated to the men who gave their lives, who paid the true price of fish on your plate.

Let us not forget their families who are left behind.

OUR BOOK VOLUNTEERS

RITA COLLIER
VOLUNTEER

I was born in brewery country, Burton on Trent, and started my working life as a scientific researcher with the National Coal Board. On marrying I moved to Porthleven and worked as a laboratory technician at Cornwall College, before taking time out to have a family. I retired in 2010 after serving Cornwall Registration Service for 28 years, working in the Helston and Penzance Offices, conducting hundreds of marriages and the first civil partnerships in Cornwall.

After working with David & Jan Penprase on two Porthleven photographic books, I was asked if I would fulfil the same role when they produced Salt of the Earth for The Fishermen's Mission. Subsequently I became a member of the committee who worked on the Porthleven Baulk Auction raising over £44,000 for the Mission.

Once again it has been a privilege to contribute to such a worthwhile project.

LAURA TYRRELL

Having recently graduated from Falmouth University in Photography. I wanted my last module to focus on something meaningful. Growing up and living in Cornwall it was a pleasure to be able to work on such an amazing Cornish project.
I found it interesting discovering the backgrounds of the fisherman and their families, the situations they go to, and have been through.
What a privilege to be a part of this fantastic book.

MELANIE KING
MANAGERESS FISHERMEN'S MISSION SHOP, HELSTON
(fourth from left)

"…a pair of original possum fur nipple warmers, but I couldn't sell them so they went to Head Office as a Secret Santa…"

I am always really proud Helston was chosen for the first and only Fishermen's Mission charity shop. I am privileged to work here. It's a very caring charity, it's obvious when you meet the Superintendents, they put their beneficiaries before everything else.

We have twenty-two volunteers and open six days a week 9.30 - 4.30. It's always busy, the public bring things in, we sort and sell it. If things don't sell the pop-up shop next door sells them for £1. Occasionally we find cash in pockets or photographs as bookmarks and we try our best to re-unite them with their owners.

It's not done to be seen more than once in the same dress at Helston Flora. We get a lot of long gowns and gorgeous hats at this time of year but with four balls a year at RNAS Culdrose there is always a market for those. The balls are themed so I try to meet demand, that's why I keep strings of beads or tea-pot lids, someone will come in and ask and we'll have one.

SARAH J BROWN (STEPHENS)
ARTIST AND FISHERMAN'S WIFE

"…I try not to worry, as most do, I've learned to box the emotions and not to worry until there's something to worry about…"

I was so excited when the first Mission shop was planned for Helston. I was asked to put something on the wall. Really honoured. It's called The Fishing Line. The shop sells second hand clothes so like families they come in all shapes and sizes. Fishermen are represented by oilers and smocks, the catches are there and the Cornish spotted scarf. The laundry prop is meant to represent the Mission, always there when things get tragic or sad propping up the families, helping to keep the line up.

My husband started fishing in Cadgwith and is now a Newlyn netter. The family boat is the Britannia IV a wooden boat built by John Moor in Mevagissey. She's been with him longer than any of his partners and we've been married twenty four years. Mainly I feel proud of him. We have short and sweet positive calls while he's at sea, it's made me very independent. I'm always ready for them to come home when going for a beer, a few beers really, and playing the Euchre league together puts it all back together again.

SANDRA PORTER
VOLUNTEER VISITOR FOR THE FISHERMEN'S MISSION
(L-R), Elizabeth Bolitho, Sandra Porter, Valerie Pill

"she was so inspiring, so wonderful, I cannot tell you how much I loved her"

We moved to Newlyn six years ago, Elizabeth Bolitho introduced me to the Mission. I'd always had a sympathy for fishermen and their hard and dangerous work in uncertain weather. Keith Dickson assessed me as being suitable for visiting.

I visit fishermen's widows and one retired fisherman. They are usually older people, with lots of stories to share who like the company. I do check sensitively if there are any questions on health or such like.

The visits are meant to last fifteen or twenty minutes. On visits to Gwynneth I'd be dragging myself away some two and a half hours or more later. She died a couple of years ago. Tales of her fascinating life as a cook when she'd argued feistily for equal pay in 1930's, or her work as a buyer for Lyons Corner Houses were so wonderful. Her rheumatoid arthritis, fourteen tablets daily, the very very serious pain would all be seen as her body letting her down. As she said 'there's nothing wrong with my brain' she was as bright as a button.

I've learned so much from the wisdom and experience of the people I visit; it is so rewarding.

THE MISSION VOLUNTEERS

KEITH DICKSON
FISHERMEN'S MISSION SENIOR SUPERINTENDENT IN CORNWALL
(back row right)

"… what the Mission uniquely gives is hope. Fishermen always thank us for the money but also for the people out there who care about them in their dark and hopeless places…"

I've worked for the Mission for eighteen years, before that I worked with the Salvation Army on the streets of Spanish Harlem, New York and in Albania. Probably the best paid job was dray driving for Carlsberg Tetley.

The Mission makes a difference, we support individuals in extremis, providing that financial security for about a month. This allows individuals to get back on their feet, get back to work or sign on for appropriate benefits. The storms of 2013/14 created desperate times for fishermen. We aim to serve and care for them, valuing them as individuals as God would; while hoping practical circumstances can and will change. That's why it's always worth the three hours of travel to get to a benefits assessment that might take minutes.

Individuals matter beyond the limited financial resources of the grants we give. Sometimes that's years of sensitive individual contact and support.

RICH STEVER
VOLUNTEER FUNDRAISER
(sixth from the right)

"…the first American to be accepted into the Mousehole Male Voice Choir since it's inception in 1909…"

I was born in Brooklyn, New York and now live in Newlyn, Cornwall. My wife is from Newlyn, we met in Baltimore, Maryland while she was nursing at Johns Hopkins University Hospital. When I retired from primary school teaching we returned to Newlyn to help look after my Mother in Law who is eighty-six and a Cornish Bard. She was a natural storyteller I loved listening to her and meeting the other Bards she introduced me to. Later I joined the Choir.

The idea was for a CD that would bring together these two themes: it is called The Voices of Cornwall: Kernow Through Story and Song. All proceeds go to The Fishermen's Mission. I asked lots of different musicians to donate a track. I recorded the Bards in my little studio at home and then gathered together recordings from a wide variety of other musicians. It is very popular we've already sold nearly a thousand.

I am keen for the Mission to develop their social media presence as a way of communicating with fishermen and the wider public. This is currently a work in progress.

Link http://voicesofcornwall.co.uk/about/

REVEREND DERATH DURKIN
VOLUNTEER

"…many Mission visitors are not Christians, the staff are, we only talk about Jesus if asked. We do try to demonstrate the love of God for everyone, be they Christian, Hindu or any other faith or none…"

About four years ago, we moved to Newlyn when I retired from full time ministry as a Church of England vicar. My role is to conduct assemblies in primary schools about the work of the Mission. In Cornwall a vast number of school children have some link with fishing, a close or distant relative or friend. Children ask some interesting questions, if I don't know the answer I know a man that can so will take a note and email the reply later. Some children I meet would not consider any other life than to fish.

When the Fishermen's Mission building closed in Newlyn we had to counter the common myth that the Mission were no longer there. The reality is the money will be more effective, supporting fishermen and not old buildings. There is still an office and re-dedicated memorial room there but activities and services we can offer across the fishing communities as a result of this change will be more appropriate to modern needs.

Printed and bound by TJ International Ltd, Padstow, Cornwall.